LETS
GO
PUBLISH

GO United States of America!

The Trump Plan Solves the Student Debt Crisis

Solution for new student debt and the existing $1.3 Trillion debt accumulation

Donald Trump in simple terms has netted out the student debt crisis from a both a student and parent perspective: "They go, and they work, and they take loans, and they're borrowed up, and they can't breathe, and they get through college and the worst thing is, they go through that whole process and they don't have any job." Trump has it right on and worse than that. They lose hope.

Trump really cares and he took the time recently to excoriate the Obama Administration and government for making it worse by making money on the student loan program: "You know the one program that the U.S. makes a whole lot of money with is student loans, and that's maybe the one program they shouldn't be making money with... "So we're going to have to start a program," he said. "We're going to do something very big with loans because you have to get these people going. They really feel down and out."

Donald J. Trump feels the pain and is going to solve the problem by refinancing, extending, better payment plans, getting universities to take some skin in the matter, and a number of other clever ways. He will address both the massive $1.3 Trillion student debt already on the books and he will work to assure that students have a chance of success and a job when they take out a college loan. It's about time. This book tells you how he plans to do it.

LETS GO PUBLISH

BRIAN W. KELLY

Copyright 2016 Brian W. Kelly   Editor, Brian P. Kelly
The Trump Plan Solves the Student Debt Crisis   Author Brian W. Kelly
Solution for new student debt and the existing $1.3 Trillion debt accumulation

Referenced Material: *The information in this book has been obtained through personal and third party observations, interviews, and copious research. Where unique information has been provided or extracted from other sources, those sources are acknowledged within the text of the book itself or at the end of the chapter in the Sources Section. Thus, there are no formal footnotes nor is there a bibliography section. Any picture that does not have a source was taken from various sites on the Internet with no credit attached. If resource owners would like credit in the next printing, please email publisher.*

Published by: LETS GO PUBLISH!
Publisher: Brian P. Kelly
Editor: Brian P. Kelly
P.O Box 621 Wilkes-Barre, PA   www.letsgopublish.com

Library of Congress Copyright Information Pending
Book Cover Design by Michele Thomas; Editing by Brian P. Kelly

ISBN Information: The International Standard Book Number (ISBN) is a unique machine-readable identification number, which marks any book unmistakably. The ISBN is the clear standard in the book industry. 159 countries and territories are officially ISBN members. The Official ISBN For this book is also on the outside cover: **978-0-9977667-9-0**

The price for this work is: **$7.99 USD**

10	9	8	7	6	5	4	3	2	1

Release Date: September 2016

Dedication

I dedicate this book to my wonderful wife Patricia; our three wonderful children Brian, Mike and Katie; and our friendly friends—Ben our very happy dog, and Buddy, our cheerful cat.

Thank You All!

Acknowledgments

I appreciate all the help that I have received in putting this book together as well as all of my other 74 published books.

My printed acknowledgments had become so large that book readers "complained" about going through too many pages to get to page one of the text.

And, so to permit me more flexibility, I put my acknowledgment list online, and it continues to grow. Believe it or not, it once cost about a dollar more to print each book.

Thank you and God bless you all for your help.

Please check out www.letsgopublish.com to read the latest version of my heartfelt acknowledgments updated for this book. Click the bottom of the Main menu!

Thank you all!

Preface:

Rarely does a book title explain exactly what a book is about. This is the exception. The Trump Plan solves the student debt crisis. It is in fact the solution for new student debt so that new high school aspirants to college do not sign up for debt when they do not need to do so. The plan also addresses how to trim to zero the $1.3 Trillion debt accumulation using some student resources and a few tricks that only a guy like Donald Trump can do.

Why did Brian W. Kelly write this book?

Brian W. Kelly wrote this book because he cares about college graduates being able to move on with their lives. I am publishing this book because I care. This book identifies the most notable and most serious flaws in student tuition financing. It then solves them by prescribing a number of Trump-unique solutions to help get the program back on track.

I hope you enjoy this book and I hope that it inspires you to take the individual action necessary to help the government of the US stand firm against any attacks on democracy from outside or from within this great country. A great way to assure a great America is to elect Donald Trump as our President.

I wish you the best.

Brian P. Kelly, Publisher
Wilkes-Barre, Pennsylvania

Table of Contents:

About the Author

Brian W. Kelly retired as an Assistant Professor in the Business Information Technology (BIT) program at Marywood University, where he also served as the IBM i and Midrange Systems Technical Advisor to the IT Faculty. Kelly designed, developed, and taught many college and professional courses. He continues as a contributing technical editor to a number of IT industry magazines, including "The Four Hundred" and "Four Hundred Guru," published by IT Jungle.

Kelly is a former IBM Senior Systems Engineer and IBM Mid Atlantic Area Specialist. His specialty was designing applications for customers as well as implementing advanced IBM operating systems and software facilities on their machines.

He has an active information technology consultancy. He is the author of 75 books and numerous technical articles. Kelly has been a frequent speaker at COMMON, IBM conferences, and other technical conferences.

Brian was a candidate for US Congress from Pennsylvania in 2010

Chapter 1   Is the Student Loan Game Rigged in Favor of Colleges and Universities?

Trump Knows!

Donald Trump can recognize a rigged game better than any man in America. He can sniff them out and call them out and /or play against them and still win. He thinks the student loan game is rigged against students and it favors the universities and the loan sharks.

Trump does not like that it is rigged and he promises to fix it. Let me ask a question about Donald Trump's opponent who could have fixed the student loan problem at some time in her thirty year political career but chose not to do so. Has Hillary Clinton to the best of your knowledge ever mentioned that the student loan game is rigged?

After thirty years in politics why has she now just come up with a few trite recommendations to solve a problem she could have had fixed years ago. Did she share any of these recent fixing thoughts with President Obama? Will they be fixed before November?

Donald Trump is the only presidential candidate who has the US student loan debt crisis solved on both fronts. His plan addresses both new student loans and the $1.3 trillion in accumulated student debt. He is serious about it and like all Trump solutions, there will be no pandering to special

2 Obama's Seven Deadly Sins

constituencies. Universities must have some skin in the game for long term solutions to be built.

Many people are affected by the crisis and so it is a topic at the dinner table in many homes—especially in those homes in which the student loan invoices are beginning to arrive for junior's or missy's four or five year sojourn into academia.

When people in the US discuss the student debt crisis, most focus on how it affects them personally. If they are not directly affected, they discuss the rapid growth in outstanding debt and its impact on the economy and the country.

They may also discuss some of the recent milestones, which are not very positive. For example, student loan debt exceeded credit card debt in 2010 and it exceeded auto loan debt in 2011. It is rapidly rising and it passed the $1 trillion mark in 2012. It is currently at about $1.3 Trillion and growing. It is a big problem. With about 27% of students defaulting on their loan paybacks mostly because the payments are so large, it is a problem for all America. Actually it is a big disgrace for a country that does not want to be labeled as "Third World."

These milestones don't tell us much about the impact of all that debt on the students themselves. They were originally made to believe by their friendly Financial Aid Officer that everybody borrows and it is a privilege to be able to attend this college with the help of the university's loan package. Sometimes as learned by default interviews, there was no up-front discussion of the loan impact. Thus, 53% of the students when graduating, did not even know there was a payback. And we all know what payback is!

70% of all college students have borrowed or still must borrow to pay for their college education. It is a national travesty. America has been told by Team Obama that we are not exceptional and the way government treats the best and the brightest, who simply are not well enough fortified to pay the huge tuition bills of today, is proof that this president and his administration were not kidding.

Meanwhile Obama has picked up $billions in profits from scobbing students with high government interest rates. No matter how immune you get to hearing about government $billions here and there, remember that a $billion is an extremely large amount of money. Even a $million is quite large. A million is so big it gives more meaning to the word billion. It is 1000 million. Would you not like to have a $million right now?

Obama's government has made the problem even worse for student loan debtors by taking more money than needed. Uncle Sam is on track to make $66 billion in profits after Uncle Obama took over the student loan program six years ago. That's why Donald Trump wants to turn the program back over to private enterprise at competitive rates.

Average student loan debt at graduation is getting larger and larger over the last two decades. In 1993-94, the average debt was just $10,000. Now, about 70% of college graduates are saddled with huge debt. Their average debt at the time they get their sheepskins is now about $35,000. It has tripled in two decades.

Graduate school debt is even worse at well over $100,000 per student. If most students were getting high paying jobs as in the past, the problem would not be as severe as students would be able to pay back the loans. Bartenders have a tough time handling Obama and Hillary approved repayment rates.

Why is student debt increasing? Government under Democrat control with grants and support for postsecondary education have simply chosen not kept pace with increases in college costs. Democrats have sold out American-born College students to gain the favor of the universities.

Government money has been diverted to welfare programs and other schemes that give Democrats advantages when they appear at fringe group events as Santa Claus. Democrats have forgotten completely about white America and the students from white America who are now saddled with huge debt repayment plans. This is not a racist thing. It simply is a bunch of overzealous white Democratic Congressmen thinking they can get the black vote by stiffing their white constituency. I am color blind but I notice things.

Colleges are oblivious as nothing has been able to hurt them. They make a ton of money while students and graduates scrounge for alms. This is their renaissance period building new theatres, art museums, student centers and all kinds of amenities to attract students and making their campuses more beautiful to the eye.

They need money to build, and heat these edifices to their success. So the burden of tuition financing has shifted much of the burden of paying for college from the federal and state governments to families. Meanwhile the drive to become the college with the finest amenities has pushed tuition charges through the roof.

Since grants and gifts and scholarships simply are not there anymore thanks to the Democrats in Congress, various types of loans in the "package" have become the primary vehicle today for high school students to make the jump to college. The government no longer carries its fair share of college costs, even though it gets a big increase in income tax revenue from college graduates who are fortunate enough to get jobs.

Ironically when the first loan bill comes to the home address; first the parents, then the students are shocked that they owe so much money and worse than that, they become convinced at the wording of the invoice that they must pay it back. Somehow, until the risk of the student withdrawing from the institution is long past, nobody from the university finds it necessary to talk about the real cost of those loans.

In the Obama economy and even for several years before, while the President had a majority Democratic Congress, family income has been flat. There is not a lot of money to pay for frills such as education. Therefore students have been forced to either borrow more to pay for college or enroll in lower-cost colleges, or forego entering an opportunity for a dream life. Without Santa Claus, work is a necessary ingredient in everything.

That shift in enrollment, from private colleges to public colleges and from four-year colleges to two-year ones, has also been responsible for a decline in bachelor's degree attainment among low- and moderate-income students. Why have Democrats in Congress who love all people not solved this? Can it be that they feel they would be helping the white privileged and they might risk reelection from their diverse constituencies?

If numbers could speak, what would they be saying?

In a recent policy paper that I read, student loan debt was defined as affordable if [Big IF] half of the after-tax increase in income that a student gains from obtaining a college degree is sufficient to repay that student's loans in 10 years or less. Nice try.

What if the student cannot get a job that uses his or her degree no matter what the student does, and they wind up being the local bartender for 20 hours per week? Before we fall off the face of the earth on that notion, let's look at what the numbers might say.

Suppose the average starting salary for a bachelor's degree recipient in the humanities discipline is about $45,000 as noted by the National Association of Colleges and Employers. That figure compares with about $30,000 in average income for high-school graduates—or a $15,000 difference.

After considering taxes, the net increase for attending college and taking all the risks is about $9,000. Half of that ($4,500) is about 10% of gross income and would be enough to repay roughly $35,000 in student loans over a 10-year repayment term. This works if the policy paper thesis is operative. It is consistent with the rule of thumb that says total student loan debt at graduation should be less than the borrower's annual starting salary.

If we accept this as a definition of affordable debt, we can analyze the data from the Baccalaureate & Beyond Longitudinal Study and we would find that the percentage of bachelor's degree recipients graduating with excessive debt grew from 9.8% in 1993-94 to 14.4% in 2007-08. Let's say the percentage has continued to grow at the same rate to today. This would suggest that 16.7% of college graduates are now graduating with excessive debt. But, it sure seems like the real percentage is a lot higher—at least according to the default rate.

Why? Part of the reason is that even this percentage underestimates the bigger problem. It includes all students who graduate with a bachelor's degree—even those without any debt at all. Suppose we were to look only at students who borrowed to attend college. It appears that more than a quarter (27.2%) of them would be and in fact are graduating with excessive debt. Some statistics show the number at closer to 30%

Can an indebted student ever get back their lives?

If President Obama had spent less time on the ill effects of white privilege and the positive purposes of black lives matter, perhaps, just perhaps, he might have had time in eight years to have analyzed and fixed the student debt problem. Maybe he thinks it is a white-only problem and white people will solve it without his help. I do not know as Obama is an enigma. What do I know? The fact is Team Obama have no ammunition at their disposal to solve any problem that presents itself with facts and/or numbers.

Even in his trusted Cabinet and his trusty Czars, which the media is no longer permitted to acknowledge, but who still exist, there are no business majors. There are no MBA's. There is nobody who knows anything about capitalism and how it really works. These pompous partial humans look down on capitalism and those trying to eke out a living in business. They innately know that they have all the knowledge as great elites always have. Why would they need to bring in an expert to solve any problem that their limited skills should dictate?

I diverted to this several paragraph diatribe because Barack Obama and Hillary Clinton are one and the same in terms of understanding business and how to make things run. If Obama and Hillary could have solved it before today, unless they hate America, they would have solved it, right?

If Donald Trump can solve it and I know he can with his proposals, how can Johnny come lately Hillary and her friend Barack claim they know anything when they did not even attempt to solve the problem for eight whole years?. Their voices on the matter are not even worth hearing.

Looking at the report introduced in the beginning of this chapter. You would soon find that students who graduate with excessive debt are about 10% more likely to say that it caused delays in their major life events, such a buying a home, getting married, or having children. They are also about 20% more likely to say that their debt influenced their employment plans, causing them to take a job outside their field, to work more than they desired, or to work more than one job.

Perhaps not surprisingly, they are also more likely to say that their undergraduate education was not worth the financial cost. Get out of town! What do universities say about that? Nobody in the corrupt press is interviewing university presidents on that subject. Why? Because the press is corrupt. But, you already knew that.

Unfortunately, there are no similar studies that can be used to analyze excessive debt for other college degrees, such as associate degrees, certificates, and graduate or professional-school degrees. It is also not possible to evaluate the financial impact of student loan debt on students who drop out of college, even though they are four times more likely to default on their loans.

There is little financial redemption for a college dropout. Maybe that is why we find them as continual lottery players or among those restricted from casinos. Looking for their big break without having a job is a losing proposition.

What Can Be Done?

Increasing national awareness of college spending is the first step in exercising restraint. Congress of course must listen to its constituents. It is therefore imperative that the federal government and the colleges and universities begin tracking the percentage of their students who are graduating with excessive debt each year. This information can then be used to improve student loan counseling if there actually is such a thing today in universities that want to be the most successful.

Colleges must also be given better tools to limit student borrowing. This is surely true. But, reality says that without federal or state insistence, would these revered institutions of higher learning even use the tools designed to help students if in so doing, they decreased their own financial opportunities to exploit student borrowers into signing up for their huge tuition packages? Most colleges and universities are aware of the problem and until now, they have checked all of their altruistic feelings at the door. One would conclude that if the college could collect one more enrollment, a little truth bending would not be excessive force.

If life were fair for example, college financial aid administrators would be permitted and in fact incented to reduce federal loan limits based on the student's enrollment status and academic major. They choose not to look at the students prospects for success because they may not get the acceptance rate they desire.

Yes, doing things against the grain would be a lot of work and it might result in less revenue for the institution. Who would suffer? Students who are enrolled half-time simply should not be able to borrow the same amount as students who are enrolled full-time. But, perhaps college officials get a little back when they sell a lucrative loan package from a private lender to a student who never even should have been admitted. Who really knows?

If colleges and universities had a student-first attitude, they would also help students better understand the debt they are taking on, by making the distinction between loans and grants clearer in their financial aid award letters. Surprise, 53% of students who get their first loan invoice did not know they owed anything? What does that's say about truth in lending? Where is the Congress? Donald Trump will solve this problem because he knows how and he loves America more than its prestigious universities.

A gentleman named Mark Kantrowitz is one of the nation's leading student financial aid experts. He is the author of a number of books written for students about paying for college. His works talk about things like Filing the FAFSA, Twisdoms about Paying for College, and Secrets to Winning a Scholarship. Mark is publisher of Cappex.com, a website that helps students achieve their college dreams, and he previously served as publisher of the FinAid, Fastweb, and Edvisors websites. So what? Well, he just gave us most of the facts in this chapter.   Thank you Mark!

Chapter 2: Solving the Student Loan Crisis and the Housing Crisis

Young people are kept down by Universities

Young and old borrowers alike owe collectively 1.3 trillion dollars of debt from their public and private student loans. With the bad economy for so long, as much as 30% of the borrowers are defaulting on their loans and this number is rising every year.

The former students simply cannot make the minimum payment. It is so bad that older students with loans are now turning 62 years of age. They get an unexpected, unwelcome surprise when their social security checks begin to be garnished by the government to pay off these old loans.

It is worse than you can imagine. My research discovered an 82 year old gentleman who once guaranteed a friend's loan and he is now paying 40% of his social security check to pay off the loan. He is left with $750 per month. Can this be America?

Many are questioning the value of a university education today when the loan brokers have to wait until retirement years to collect the debt from government payments intended to sustain life.

Students in the bottom 60% of the class have lower prospects for work in their chosen field. One after another are wishing they could have that loan decision they made at 17 or 18 years old back again for a do over. It would never happen.

They now know their huge loans; many over $100,000 may very well ruin their lives. Nobody offered counselling on student debt and the negative impact it would have on the lives of so many of our young in America. Over 70% of graduates are on the hook to pay off student loans.

Where are the good jobs promised by the Universities for all the money borrowed? At the same time that most graduates cannot get jobs, the jobs they do get pay less. The average salary of college graduates has gone down 10% in the past few years while inflation is growing at an ever faster clip.

Moreover, 85% of college graduates from 2011 have had to swallow their pride and move home with mom and dad because they could not afford life on their own. It doesn't take a rocket scientist to call out: Houston, we have a problem!

Meanwhile nobody is talking about the Universities permitting more and more foreign students into their programs. When they graduate; guess whose jobs they take? A major source of H-1B visas (college graduates) is international students from U.S. university campuses.

The reason corporations hire them before Americans is they are a ready source of cheap labor. Universities not only sell their foreign national graduates to corporations, they also hire more than their fair share of professors from the foreign national community--many of these have just received graduate degrees (PhD's) from American Universities

They fire existing faculty and replace them with younger foreign national professors willing to work for less money. I know because I was fired from Marywood University during a cost-cutting restructuring and my replacement had recently graduated from the University of Alexandria in Egypt. Marywood did not open up his employment dossier to me but what seems to be is most often what is.

Smaller Universities will even outsource the legal part of the visa work to assure the foreign applicant a six-year H-1B visa. They will contract with immigration law firms and pay up to $10,000 or more per faculty member depending on the complexity of the case for the purpose of hiring a new faculty member who will work cheap.

Do cheap foreign speaking non-citizen faculty have any effect on the quality of education our children receive? Trying to figure out what was just said is too common in today's classrooms.

It is really tough for Americans to get hired in US Universities since our Congress permits an unlimited number of foreign nationals to be hired as professors or staff at US Universities. Additionally, colleges also love to hire part timers at about 1/10 the pay rate as full-timers. Meanwhile why are graduating students not getting jobs to help them pay off their student debt?

With more and more former students not being able to survive without their parents, this also has an impact on the student borrower's ability to ever break away. Purchasing a home is out of the question as the college loan is already bigger than the mortgage would be. This is already having a major effect on the housing market and it will continue for years to come. Who will buy the new homes if not the young?

No solution is simple. With about 30% or more former students ultimately defaulting on their loans, and many more trapped in a financial abyss from which they can never escape, Congress can certainly create a better way to help the borrower, the housing market, and the taxpayer, all at the same time.

I would suggest that Congress assure that in times when saving earns just a percent or two interest, student lenders first have their interest rates capped at something that is well out of the usury category. Students are in crisis mode in their lives while protected lenders never had it so good.

A Progressive Loan Payback Schedule

Without getting very complicated, I would recommend putting together a progressive payback schedule (like the progressive income tax) based on adjusted gross income. Every borrower with income or receiving on government payments should have to pay something. Nobody should pay less than 1% of their income. But paying 90% of income towards loan debt makes graduates soon decide to default.

I would start the maximum rate of payment at 5% for the lowest income borrowers and then take it up to 15% for those in default who are doing quite well. Of course in no instance would anybody have to pay more than the minimum monthly payment for the loan even if they could afford it.

To help pay for the program, I would also set up a fund for any taxpayer to check off from $1.00 up to any amount on their tax forms to have part of their refund directed towards the paying down of all student loans. We do this for campaign donations so why not for student loans. I have other recommendations and the following may be considered somewhat controversial.

Colleges do not suffer at all

All of this money that former students have paid and will pay over the years has already gone into the bulging coffers of universities across the nation, who seemingly have no skin in the game. They got paid for their "service" up front and are never asked to look back. They have pocketed the money for many students of their students who have not gotten a job and perhaps never will be been able to get a job—ever.

And, since the products of the universities, the students, as a rule have not been able to achieve the American dream as promised by the Admissions Counselors, and since such Universities encourage foreign students to take jobs in the US upon graduation and they hire foreign faculty when Americans are available, Universities cannot be left out of the solution. Yes, it should cost them until they start being more realistic and accountable.

Their admission departments and "loan" departments have actually created the problem as half of the graduating students are unaware that they have debt from a loan or several loans that they signed years earlier. Universities are a part of the problem. In this regard, I would ask the Congress to enact legislation to make them part of the solution, providing the following:

1. Based on their student default rate, collect a fee of 5% of gross revenue to 15% (same rates as student payback) that is applied to paying down all student loans. The minimum payment would be a factor of the default rate for the institution and the percentage of gross revenue. The exact formula will need some work.

2. Limit the number of foreign students until the unemployment rate is 3% and cap the number permitted to obtain work visas after graduation to a small / reasonable number.

3. Limit the number of H-1B visas for faculty to a very small number-- 5%. It is currently unlimited.

4. Assure the H-1B faculty member on worker visa returns to the home country after 6 years. Worker visas do not get in line for green card or citizenship.

5. Reduce all non-University H-1B visas from 85,000 or whatever the limit is du jour by 90% until the unemployment rate goes to 3%.

6. Come up with a payment plan in addition to the above in which a certain percentage, say 5% of the endowment is used to pay off student debt. To make it fair, this also would be based on the default rate for the institution. For those who do not understand the notion of an endowment, it is typically a large fund that is amassed by universities and other institutions from the kind donations / bequeathals of dedicated alumni.

The dollars in university endowments are staggering and could pay off the country's entire student debt. For example, Harvard University alone, with its 380 years' worth of alumni to hit up, boasts an endowment of $36 billion. Apple

Inc.'s famously large cash hoard is just $21 billion. Yes, Harvard has more cash than Apple while students are in loan default trying to pay off their Harvard loans. Both Yale University and Stanford University's endowments are also larger than Apple's cash hoard, and Princeton University is not too far behind.

7. **The Trump Plan**. Use 5% of the proceeds from the Trump plan to balance the budget and pay off the entire student debt. Just 5% will pay off the entire student debt load in eight years. Put all students with forgiveness on a plan in which they pay 5% of their income for ten years and then they are debt free. Of course if their debt is paid sooner, ten years is not necessary.

By the way, many big Brainiac economists who have mastered our terrible economic performance in the past eight do not like the Trump plan for the national debt. They should be ignored. They have already proven they cannot handle the job.

As president, Donald Trump is considering selling off $16 trillion worth of U.S. government assets in order to fulfill his pledge to eliminate the national debt in eight years, senior adviser with the campaign Barry Bennett said. How about adding another $1.3 trillion to the repayment plans to handle student debt.

"The United States government owns more real estate than anybody else, more land than anybody else, more energy than anybody else," Bennett announced. "We can get rid of government buildings we're not using, we can extract the energy from government lands, and we can do all kinds of things to extract value from the assets that we hold."

In a wide-ranging interview with The Washington Post, Trump said he would get rid of the $19 trillion national debt "over a period of eight years."

8. Use Trump's America-First Fossil Fuel Plan. Take a nice cut from opening up all US oil lands. While headlines have reported declining oil, gas, and coal prices, those declines do not deter from the fact that U.S. energy resources are valuable to our domestic economic growth. It is documented that the US now has the most energy reserves in the entire world.

The most recent government estimate of those benefits was a 2012 Congressional Budget Office (CBO) study, produced at the request of the House Budget Committee, which analyzed federal lease revenues that could be expected to arise from a proposal to open federal lands and waters to oil, gas, and coal extraction. Donald Trump is ready to bring this in right away and it will more than pay for outstanding student debt. Remember we need $1.3 trillion to pay it all off. Look at the results from the US study below:

GDP increase:

- ✓ $127 billion annually for the next seven years.
- ✓ $663 billion annually in the next thirty years.
- ✓ $20.7 trillion cumulative increase in economic activity over the next thirty-seven years.

These estimates include "spillover" effects, or gains that extend from one location to another location. For example, increased oil production in the Gulf of Mexico might lead to more automobile purchases that would increase economic activity in Michigan.

Spillover effects would add an estimated $69 billion annually in the next seven years and $178 billion over thirty years.

Jobs increase:

- ✓ 552,000 jobs annually over the next seven years.
- ✓ Roughly 2.7 million jobs annually over the next thirty years.

Jobs gains would be not only in fields directly related to oil, gas, and coal but more than 75% of the jobs would be in high-wage, high-skill employment like health care, education, professional fields, and the arts.

Wage increase:

- ✓ $32 billion increase in annual wages over the next seven years.
- ✓ $163 billion annually between seven and thirty years.
- ✓ $5.1 trillion cumulative increase over thirty-seven years.

Increase in tax revenue:

- ✓ $3.9 trillion increase in federal tax revenues over thirty-seven years.

✓ $1.9 trillion in state and local tax revenues over thirty-seven years.
✓ $24 billion annual federal tax revenue over the next seven years, $126 billion annually thereafter.
✓ $10 billion annual state and local tax revenue over the next seven years, $61 billion annually thereafter.

Why does Hillary's plan ignore these facts?

✓ She did not think of it
✓ She hates fossil fuels like oil and gas and coal
✓ She hates corporations that create jobs

If she had another good thought, it would be lonesome

Chapter 3 Congress Treats Student Loans Like It's Your Kid; Not Their Kid!

One would think we elected buffoons

If we did not elect them, that is what we got anyway. There ought to be enough money in the federal budget to hire experts. Donald Trump and every other successful business mogul runs their businesses with experts to make a buck. Nobod does it alone and nobody hires the second team to do the job. How could our legislators be as ambivalent on something as simple as the interest rates for student loans?

History of student loan interest rates

Let's take a look at the tumultuous history of student loan interest rates. At best it is characterized by bipartisan indecision, delayed legislation and temporary solutions. Congress gets a solid "F" grade for this performance. At worst, the government hired workers with the lowest IQ's to figure this out.

Understanding the events is key to knowing Congress's thinking on interest rates' current trajectory. Here's a quick summary of the last 20 years in student loans. This information was gleaned from the New America Foundation.

1992-93: (6.94%) Variable interest rates are introduced for federal student loans.

1993-94: (6.22%) Congress creates the direct loan program to gradually eliminate the need for bank loans.

1994-95: (7.43%) The variable rate maximum drops from 9% to 8.25%.

1998-99: (7.46%) The interest rate change set to begin in 1998 is postponed another five years. C

2001-02: (5.99%) The scheduled 2003 alterations become a topic of debate. Student advocates defend the change.

2002-03: (4.06%) The 1993 rate change is canceled. The current variable rate remains in place. In 2006, loans will begin to carry a 6.8% fixed interest rate. 2005-06: (5.3%) With the 6.8% fixed rate in place, Congress launches a campaign pledge to cut student loan interest rates in half.

2007-08: (6.8%) Making good on the pledge, Congress passes a bill for a temporary 4 yr. interest rate reduction.

2008-09: (6% for Subsidized Stafford, 6.8% for other loans)

2010-11: (4.5% for Subsidized Stafford, 6.8% of other loans) Third phase of rate cuts, Congress eliminates the bank-based federal student loan program.

2011-12: (3.4% for subsidized Stafford, 6.8% for other loans) The fourth and final phase of temporary rate cut.

2012-13: (6.8%) The 2007 rate reduction expires on July 1, 2012 and rates revert to 6.8%.

Apr. 27, 2012: The House passes bill to extend the 3.4% interest rate.

2015-2016: (4.29%)

2016-2017: (3/76%)

Follow the bouncing ball…

Assigning student graduates to debtor's prison

Raising the loan rates as the federal government did is mid-year 2012 for Stafford Loans helped about as much as putting all the student debt laggards, many from our own families, in a debtor's prison. This is not part of my solution.

About Seven million students had enjoyed "reduced rate" Stafford loans to help them get through college. The interest rate on these loans was scheduled to double on July 1, 2012. It is going from 3.4 percent to 6.8 percent unless Congress acts. Congress let the rates go up.

The House had already passed the necessary legislation to do so and the Senate was planning a similar action. This would raise costs by an average of $1,000 each, according to the White House. While many students are already in default, a thousand dollar increase surely was not expected to help them pay their loan off any quicker.

When students default, it is not good. In some cases, they ruin their lives, and it costs us all. Ask yourself why interest rates are so high on student loans. They are higher than mortgages. How is that? Ask Congress! Who makes that interest? Who pockets it? The government scobs our kids a high rate while offering less than a percent on deposits. How is that fair?

Students with a debt of $100,000 or more, and there are more and more and more of them, face payments well over $1,000 per month. That is tough to pay when you are unemployed. It is tough to pay if you are on Social Security. That is why over 5 million student borrowers have already defaulted and more default every day.

For your edification, it helps to know somebody is making a killing on this interest and it is not you or I. The National Student Loan Debt Clock raises 2,726 dollars per second according to Market Watch 2016.

When I paid off my National Defense Student Loan (NDSL) in the 1970's, my payments were just over $10.00 per month. I paid it off as soon as I could as it was an annoyance. I also had a PA State low-interest loan and its payments were closer to $25.00 per month. It took a little longer to pay this off but by the time I was married at 27 years old, all of my student loan debts were paid.

This is not possible today. Back then, the government was not interested in sending young men and women into debtor's prison or making them dependents of government for life.

Today's students are looking at big payments for a long, long time and while they are making those payments, they are postponing serious relationships, postponing starting a family, and postponing buying a new home. They simply cannot afford it and the more oppressive the government makes payback terms, the more likely student borrowers will simply give-up. That surely does not help the US taxpayers or those who build homes for a living. Of course, we can throw all these young bums in jail?

Can Mighty Mouse save us all? "Here I come to save the day… that means that Mighty Mouse is on his way!" Don't count on it but the Mighty Obama has taken his swipe at the problem and it has been recorded.

On Oct. 26, 2011 President Obama decided to save the world—again. He came out with a new initiative that would allow student borrowers to cap their loan repayments at 10 percent of their discretionary income starting sometime in 2012. The effect of Obama's directive was that the effective date was two years earlier than the same act that was passed by Congress. Obama likes doing things without Congress.

In October 2011, ABC reported that Obama said: "We can't wait for Congress to do its job. So where they won't act, I will." Upon inspection, unfortunately, as well intentioned as it might have been, the Obama plan does not help those who already had student loans (pre 2008) and had graduated or left school. In other words most of the students with the problem were not part of this solution.

Donald Trump and I have a better plan than Obama's for potential borrowers and at the end of this book, you will see that this is a solution for those student borrowers and their parents who are already stuck in the mire.

Should I go to College?

It is a tough question to answer nowadays. Unless you are convinced that you can at a minimum be in the top 25% of your class, and you are willing to work unbelievably hard to assure your class rank, you are better off trying to get a job right now and forego college temporarily.

Do not go to college full-time. You are the only one taking a risk that it will help you in the future. if it does not, you may be strangled by debt. If you do not graduate or others beat you big time in the class-rank area, you will suffer all your life for the mistake. I would suggest taking a few courses at a time in your spare time and in the summer. Do not take out any student loans. Ever! Save your life so you can be free.

When a reader named Sue commented on the ABC report of Obama's initiative on their News site, she offered the best advice I have seen in a long time to assure new students that are not now swamped by student debt, to avoid ever getting into the big student borrowing hole. Sue responded with tremendous insight into the real problem today with student loans – the 800 pound gorilla in the room that nobody wants to talk about in an honest way.

In Sue's words: "I actually don't believe that we should put a college education in everyone's hands and think that line of thinking is part of the problem with education in this country." Sue continues:

"For decades we've restructured our elementary and high school systems to become one-size-fits-all and college is quickly going that route too. But the reality is that not everyone fits the mold. Not everyone is cut out for an office job and not everyone is cut out for construction. In some communities, we are now seeing a return to skills training in high schools, where kids can graduate from high school with a two year business degree from the local community college and a cosmetology license, or a mechanics license as well as their high school diploma.

"These are kids who can go right from high school into the work force with the training they need, start working (or start their own business from their parent's garage). They won't be saddled with student loans.

The President's program of encouraging students to go into debt (sorry, but a student loan is a debt) to get an education is backwards – and in the end, not everyone needs a college education to move the country forward, they simply need to be trained to do what they want to do, and preferably, they should learn it in high school."

Sue has a head on her shoulders for sure.

Who in a debtor's prison ever earned enough to gain their freedom? More and more student borrowers who are already in a debtor's prison see the invisible bars, and choose to escape in the only way they know how. They stop paying even a dime and they stop answering their phone.

They see their student debt as hopeless. After a few reprieves, a few thousand 8 AM phone calls that wake up mom and dad, several forbearances, with their debt climbing through the roof, they give up and call it quits. For a while before the end, they believe they are paying for the right to remain out of default, in much the same way they would if the dollars were borrowed from a loan shark.

But, when the balance goes up as the checks go out, they finally reach a point where the alternative is a better alternative. They default on their loans. Five million and growing have done this so far.

There are those successful and somewhat lucky graduates who are not suffering from the pain of this huge debt since they have the means or the jobs to pay off their loans. I have read their comments. Though they are in the minority, many of them are indignant that the others, not so lucky should get a small break, and surely not a big break. They have little compassion for those who do not pay their bill even if they have no job.

From the Internet chatter on student loans, many that are doing well do not think that their university peers should even ask taxpayers to help them pay off their loans as it would be unfair to those, such as the fortunate with jobs, who are paying or who have paid their loans off on time.

This is surely understandable and I would agree that these debts should not be forgiven. But, it would be a good idea for those in default, those about to default, and those who ultimately will have to pay for the default to consider making the debt more able to be paid. Nobody gains a few years after default, when the debt is rendered uncollectible and the once hopeful student's life is basically ruined for good.

None of us will get in line to give what is not needed to the poor, but most will help as much as we can. From talking to the parents of students in default, I can assure you that no parent, who in good faith sent their children to higher education institutions that promised the world, expected less of a life in return. Nobody expected the world but nobody expected a life of misery after gaining the coveted degree. Meanwhile, the university long ago has cashed all the checks even though their degree in many cases is worthless to the graduate.

At the bottom of the student debt issue today is that colleges and universities oversold their product. The dike is still leaking as they are still able to do this with impunity. You find no big stories about colleges being punished for not doing a good job. They should be punished by helping their student graduates with their loan repayments.

Not learning from their mistakes, universities create a never ending lines of students heading for the debtors prison. These one-time students often get no chance at stopping for a brief while just to have a life, a house, a husband, or a child.

Without assurances of a top class rank, no sane parent, properly advised by a school or a compassionate government, would have encouraged their children to take out huge school loans approaching a hundred thousand dollars after four or five years unless they knew something good was going to happen.

In the end, they see their children with a worthless education and a worthless piece of paper to hang on the wall. Now that the results are in, and there are over five million defaults equaling five million ruined lives, what sane parent should consider signing up their children today with the same risk of ruining their lives?

Only the colleges and universities benefit and it is time that they get called on it. It is far better to be unemployed without a huge debt than to be unemployed and be heading to the veritable debtor's prison until the loan is paid off.

Many parents expected and some still believe that the very act of going to college should result in guaranteed success. The success would include a good job for the graduate and thus there would be a means of paying for the education. Even more importantly, paying off the loan is a side show on the ladder of success, but having the means to buy a home and have a better life—that is the piece d' resistance!

Today, unfortunately, as parents have found, the verdict is in. Those dreams are not ever going to materialize. Worse than that; those parents who were duped by the admissions counselors in the fancy suits witnessed their children being set up for a life of future miserableness that might just as well be a debtor's prison. I am afraid it is that bad.

Go to the Internet and type in student loan repayments and you can see the despair and the disappointment expressed by the victims of the student loan charade. If you think the credit card issue with young people is bad, consider that Congress decided that with student loans, your children can get no relief at all—ever.

Shall we say the loan sharks / lobbyists and their accomplices in the colleges and universities convinced Congress to act in such a way that does not help students who are merely trying to better themselves? I think you can win a bet on that one.

The irony is that colleges and universities are mum about the problem as if they have no culpability at all. These institutions have become in many ways like the bad businesses listed by the Better Business Bureau. Ironically, in recent years, as a recruiting tool, colleges and universities, especially those that operate mostly online, have found a need to register with the Better Business Bureau. Moreover, they use their listing to prove their worthiness to students.

The truth is as missing from their work as it is from Hillary Clinton's defense of her emails.

Better Business Bureau certified

For the Better Business Bureau, legitimate proof of success for a college or university to produce is simply that they actually do bestow degrees. Degrees ae simply pieces of paper if somebody does not respect the supposed meaning of the paper.

The degree of course is intended to represent the end of a major higher educational process that provides the knowledge for one to be successful in their area of study. When presented in the form of a sheepskin or a rolled piece of paper, for the BBB, that is proof positive that the university is not in a scam business.

When I wrote an article about this debtor's phenomenon in 2012, I was misinformed. I wrote this: "But, does it really provide the proper proof? Are the universities of today, where 85% of American graduates in 2011 were so inadequately prepared for life that they had to go back home for sustenance, really worthy of being heralded by the Better Business Bureau as bastions of opportunity."

My apologies to those who bought my "facts" back then. The bogus 85 percent figure that CNN, Time and The New York Post breathlessly reported that year was incorrect. The number is 45 percent. Forty-Five percent is still high. This number also is a report card on universities and it means that 45% of their job placements did not succeed.

It does not take parents long to determine that the real proof of success, a proof not even asked for by the BBB, is the percentage of students that are employed in their major field. These statistics are even more dismal.

Yet, the colleges and universities continue to be in good standing? Something is wrong in America. An employed college graduate counts as employed even if they are tossing pizza dough at the Hut or tossing burgers on the grille at McDonalds, while waiting impatiently for the minimum wage to be raised to $15.00 per hour.

Let me repeat my thesis please. The vendor that provides the no value education—the college or university—is not held accountable for its failure to produce a functioning product. Of course the finished products are graduates that more often than not nowadays are not at all capable of gaining the promises extended.

Parents remember when the students were courted by the Admissions Department, and the Financial Aid Department, and all questions were answered in the positive.

Four or five years prior, these students and their parents were asked to sign letters of intent and even the more important quickie student loan applications to permit them to matriculate. Other papers in the pile included their loan applications, already filled out but for the signature. There was no guarantee form within the mass of paperwork, though the guarantee was even more than implied.

Worse than that, as if the student loan travesty has never happened, these same charlatans, dressed in their university plumage and finery are permitted each and every year to continue to solicit and encourage a fresh batch of vulnerable 18-year olds to step into the financial abyss of a life that they will never be permitted to begin. And the institutions do so with vigor and complete impunity.

As a former college professor retired in 2011, I know that many parents and student graduates today are questioning the value of their university education. They have good reason to do so. When the loan brokers have to wait until retirement years to collect the debt from social security or unemployment payments, can we all not admit that something is woefully wrong in America. Why would we encourage more of a bad thing?

The Obama Administration produces no really good jobs for fresh college graduates. Any jobs that are created are given to international student visa holders by the same universities that helped our children underachieve. Should the colleges and universities be able to take credit for job placements when the lucrative fields in which the graduate is placed includes areas of endeavor such as bartenders, waiters/waitresses, truck drivers, or other blue collar type jobs? Do the parents credit the University for these types of job placements—especially for graduate students? I think not.

From what I see from being in the front line, students in the bottom 25% of their class have about zero prospects for work in their field. Those in the bottom 60% have a small chance. Most in these circumstances wish they could have that student loan decision, which they made at 17 or 18 years of age back again for a do-over.

What great decisions did you make when you were seventeen or eighteen? Now, you know the extent of the problem. Student borrowers eventually learn that their huge loans, many over $100,000, may very well ruin their lives. For them, before they realize a modicum of success, they find their life has become a veritable debtors' prison, a dead end for someone the world is ready to call a *deadbeat,* despite the sheepskin hanging on the wall.

Where are the good jobs promised by the universities for all the money borrowed? At the same time that most graduates cannot find jobs, the jobs they do find pay less and less— even if it is in their chosen field. The average salary of college graduates has gone down 10% in the past few years while inflation is growing at an ever faster clip. This is caused by a combination of a poor economy and because foreign graduates holding student visas take American jobs right after graduation.

It helps to again offer the starkest statistic of all so all Americans understand this problem is not going away by itself. Forty-Five percent (not 85%) of college graduates from 2011 have had to swallow their pride and move home with mom and dad because they cannot afford life on their own. CNN had once reported the number at 85%. It doesn't take a rocket scientist to call out: "Houston, we have a problem!"

I must admit that I am surprised that nobody is calling out the universities for permitting more and more foreign students into their programs and then helping them gain employment ahead of American students. When foreign students graduate; guess whose jobs they take? According to their student visas, they are supposed to return to their country of origin. Once in America, however, they are not about to leave.

There are many groups that help students on their quest for employment in the US after graduating from an American university. Many students come to America to stay and so they must be employed in order to remain legally in the country. Then again, the illegal residency option is also used when students cannot find jobs in their two-month opportunity period.

International Students taking American jobs is a big problem for American students trying to get a job. Ask the university placement office for the statistics on foreign student placements and for American student placements. Do not let them include the few students who go home in the denominator. Do not let them appear like it is not a problem for you.

In their senior year, the very same universities and pillaging law firms line up to represent foreign students. They make recommendations for those who want to stay in America and not go home as required by the terms of their student visas—to which they agreed and swore. International students can take any of these four options:

✓ Enroll in the Optional Practical Training (OPT) and work in the United States for a year
✓ Get an H-1B (high tech work visa) to work at an American organization
✓ Attend graduate school in the US while working on gaining employment
✓ Simply do not go home and work underground
✓ Whereas we most often refer to these as foreign students; the universities like refer to them as International Students. Watch that trick designed to get American students to think less of themselves because they are not "international."!

How can a foreigner get a job in America after graduation as an International Student? There are a number of answers. Starting from the beginning, a student living in the US with an F-1 or J-1 (student) visa has 60 days to either enroll in another college or university for graduate studies or they can enroll in the OPT program to gain employment.

The *OPT* program is a very good deal for foreign students but not such a good deal for American students. It permits the J-1 and F-1 student visa status to be extended for one year so that the International student can gain professional training in their area of direct study. The application can take three to four months, so most students are advised early in their senior year to begin the process so that at graduation time, they may continue to stay in the country with employment. Their employment, by the way, may very well be the same job for which your son or daughter was aspiring. But, nobody is counting the Americans who are hurt by such programs.

So, after completing all course requirements for the degree, foreign students can gain full-time employment with American companies for one year. During that year, they can work to gain an H-1B visa for the following six years. This gives up to six additional years and then they can look to extend the H-1B again or work with their company sponsor to help them gain a green card, which is non-citizen, permanent residency in the US. Meanwhile our children who demand a living wage, are waiting for the USCIS to send these job poachers home. But, they never do!

Between 2009 and 2010, as less and less Americans students were being hired, the number of *OPT* students employed in American jobs rose by 14.43 percent.

Overall, if foreign students opt to stay in the US for a longer period of time, they simply get a company to sponsor them for the H-1B non-immigrant visa. This allows them to remain employed at that company for three years, and then they can get that extended for up to six or more years.

So, as the problem for young American student graduates gaining employment comes into focus, we see that a major destination for foreign students is the American workplace by achieving H-1B visas (college graduate – supposedly hi-techs).

International students from US university campuses are prime candidates for these positions. So, an innocent college education for a foreign student winds up being a job killer for American students. Yes, they do work for less. I know!

It is our Congress that permits this to occur by passing laws that are unfair to American citizens. And so, we find foreign graduates with degrees from the same universities as our children applying for jobs at the same companies that would hire our children if they were willing to work under the same conditions and for the same reduced wages as the foreign students. Once an employer is found, the H-1B visa is granted and the foreign graduate takes the job for typically six years. Meanwhile American students go home to Mom and Dad simply to survive.

In other words, F-1, and J-1 visa holders are supposed to go home but they find university counselors or university lawyers to help get the deck stacked in their favor. They either use the OPT program or they go right to the H-1B visa program so they do not have to go home. Because they do not go home, your children cannot get jobs. Any questions?

The reason corporations hire foreigners over Americans is not because they are superior students but that they are a ready source of cheaper, yet still highly competent labor. Universities not only sell their foreign national graduates to corporations; they also hire more than their fair share of professors from the foreign national community. That is how I lost my own job so I know.

Many of those hired in universities have just received graduate degrees from American universities. In other words, for financial and diversity reasons, the universities prefer not to hire Americans for the faculty jobs, which they have available. Students are taught American subjects by foreigners who can hardly speak the American language – English!

Congress permits colleges and universities to hire an unlimited number of foreigners as faculty or staff with the H-1B visa program. It is the exception to the nominal 65,000 visas permitted each year. American colleges and universities have a vested interest in foreign students and foreign workers. Ironically, they have no such interest in Americans, who pay their salaries.

I have witnessed universities firing existing faculty to replace them with younger foreign national professors willing to work for less money. Smaller universities will even outsource the legal part of the visa work to assure the foreign applicant a six-year H-1B visa. They will contract with immigration law firms and pay up to $10,000 or more per faculty member depending on the complexity of the case for the purpose of hiring a new faculty member who will work cheap for the sake of the university. How does this help American students?

Do you think that a "cheap" faculty has any effect on the quality of education our children receive? It is really tough for Americans to get hired in US Universities since our Congress has seen fit to permit an unlimited number of foreign nationals to be hired as professors or staff at universities of all sizes in the US.

With more and more debt saturated former students not being able to survive without their parents, this also has an impact on the indebted jobless student borrower's ability to ever consider purchasing a home. I know I said this already but it is how it is!

This is already having a major effect on the housing market and it will continue for years to come. Who will buy the new homes if not the young? How can a college graduate that owes the equivalent of a huge house in student loan debt, ever be considered for purchasing a home? One problem will continue to feed the other until the student debt crisis is solved. Then, homes will again be sold in America at the proper sale amount.

No solution is simple. With 30% or more former students ultimately defaulting on their loans, and many more trapped in a financial abyss (a debtor's prison more or less), from which they may never escape, Congress can certainly create a better way to help the borrower, the housing market, and the taxpayer, all at the same time. It might not benefit foreigners or the universities but it would help parents and the students that got sucked into promises from university pitchmen that are as powerful as the best infomercials you have ever seen on TV.

What is the Solution?

We have already discussed a number of solutions. Government must act now. Short of debtor's prison, I would suggest that Congress assure that in times when no person in the US can find a savings account earning more than a percent (or two) interest rate; that the student lenders should not be able to inflict usury rates on students. This is common practice today and it leads many student borrowers to default. Why should students pay 6% to 10% while they can earn only 1%? Is the government trying to hurt student Americans?

Student borrowers need to have their interest rates capped at something that is affordable. What food does it do if 27% default today and 50% default ten years from now?

I would like Congress to help me understand why the Stafford Loan interest percentage should be raised to almost 7% when only a rare bank pays more than one percent interest. When today's borrowers can get a mortgage for just over 4%, and the best savings rate that the most lucrative banks give is less than 1.5%, why would our government ever permit the Stafford loan or any loan for that matter to be so much higher than the savings interest rate.

On the Sallie Mae Web Site, they advertise an APR of 9.72% for new student loans. This is ridiculous unless you run a government funded debtor's prison, or your background is the loan shark business.

Nobody wants defaults on these loans or any other loans but the terms have become so usurious and oppressive that the law of unintended consequences is beginning to deal many defaults right from the top of the deck. This must be solved post haste.

As we are all aware, Congress has taken the bankruptcy option off the table for students so for many, there is no way out of the hole. There is not even a speck of light at the end of the tunnel. Is this really what we want or would we fashion a solution that brings back some hope to what is now a situation that makes many of our young citizens either actually hopeless or feeling hopeless. Tell me the difference?

After assuring very low, reasonable, payback interest rates, just a hair above the Treasury note, I would recommend Congress make the student loan game fair again by rounding in the student borrower's favor rather than the lender. Simply trace back the last few iterations of legislation and instead of making students targets of corrupt lenders, strip those lenders of the powers that the Congress has given them.

Let me offer some examples:

Most of the laws enacted by Congress have hurt those who do not have the means to pay back their student loans at the rate demanded by Sallie Mae or other legitimate "loan sharks" in the student loan industry. For example, Congress enacted the 2005 Bankruptcy Abuse Prevention and Consumer Protection Act, which presupposes that students; who are in fact bankrupt, can be enslaved in a debtor's prison and through prayer, and perhaps some great prison poker skills, can somehow come up with the money to pay off their student loans.

This gift from Congress had a number of sweet surprises for students, who at the time were looked upon as the bad guys! The big surprise is that Student loans that were not guaranteed by the federal government were henceforth deemed to not be eligible to be discharged in bankruptcy. This became law on October 17, 2005. In other words, when credit card companies find out that you used your credit card to pay for a course, they can come after you under the law.

Would any American think that the laws for credit card debt would be less severe than the laws for students trying to gain an American education? What limitations are there on credit card purchases? They can be used for anything. Student loans can be used only for education, so why would

Congress treat credit card debt in a more favorable light than student debt?

Additionally, to show its utter disdain for students who cannot get jobs and are forced to default, Congress changed the Higher Education Act and eliminated all statutes of limitations for the collection of student loan debt – even those from the past.

So, out of nowhere, students who once had a tough time paying off their loans in times of leniency on student debt, which had passed the time specified in the statute of limitations, and who were thus free from their debt in the 70's and 80's, again found themselves getting billed for the forgiven debt. Again their arrearage plus their remaining debt amount became a collectible debt! But for them, they became outlaws as their debt remained uncollectible.

And we know how nice the collectors are when they call at 7 or 8 in the AM.

Here is another goodie. The law now permits lenders to lie about student loans and it is OK! Yes, Student loans are specifically exempted from coverage under the Truth in Lending Act (TILA). They are also now specifically exempted from state usury laws...lending money at an unreasonably high interest rate.

If the student loan sharking agencies raise the rate to 55%, you must pay the rate. Additionally, most student loan guarantors do not have to adhere to the 1988 Federal Trade Commission legislation requiring an adherence to Fair Debt Collection and Practices in pursuing defaulted borrowers.

Why not? With over 5 million students in default, and parents more and more involved in the game, how does this help anybody? Are the debt collectors included in the private industry job gains the Administration likes to claim? Can we do with fewer of these types in society?

Please do not get the wrong idea. There were days in which students graduated and then laughed at the idea of paying back their student loans and eventually the loan went away. These are not those days and these are not the debtors of which I speak. I am talking about our kids.

I am not looking for a return to those days but the pendulum has gone too far the other way and Congress must fix it. People are getting hurt in many ways and I read just today of a young lady with stage 2 curable cancer who was being hounded so much by student loan debt collectors that she took her own life. I am sure there are more situations like this.

Is this what we really want for America? Should we punish our young when they are young, and then expect them to grow up to treat the world fairly?

Anybody who checks what the student lenders are doing, and how harshly they treat everybody—people who do not have two nickels to rub together—would admit that somehow a big sin has been perpetrated against the youth in America and our Federal Government not only permits it; it encourages it!

Seventeen and eighteen year olds signing up for a life in a debtor's prison is a sin just like the children, just over ten years old, working in the mines prompted the child labor laws.

So, let's solve the problem in a fair way that does not take the life out of the most alive people in America—our children. The recommended solution keeps income flowing to repay the loans and gets the loan sharking, unfair collection tactics, and garnishment of social security out of the student loan business. It is worth a hard look.

The first step is to stop additional student loan abuse. It is not always best for students to go to college. Getting a position as a truck driver, five years after high school, with a college degree and a huge debt does not help anybody but the university. Getting that job five years earlier helps a part-time student immensely.

Let's bring back the Kuder tests to check aptitude in high school and stop the insistence that everybody needs to complete their life by having gone to some college someplace at some time. Unless you can afford the $100,000 and expect nothing in return, stay away from College scene unless again, you are convinced that you will be in the top 25%.

First of all, I recommend giving all the defaulted student borrowers a second chance at making it right. That brings five million lost participants back into the game. If each give just one dollar a year, that is $5 million more dollars than would have arrived otherwise. Everything counts. Let's ask for more!

Every student borrower with current income should have to pay something back on their loan but it cannot be the equivalent of being in a debtor's prison. I recommend a progressive payback schedule (like the progressive income tax) based on adjusted gross income.

Up to the poverty line, let's set the percentage at 1% so everybody pays something against their debt. Set the minimum rate of payment in the schedule after the poverty line at 5%. Yes, everybody pays something. I would suggest a bracket for each 5% up to a maximum rate of 25% of income for the highest bracket.

Let's look at a typical IRS schedule. The 2012 tax brackets will suffice to get an idea on how to structure this:

Tax Bracket Single
10% Bracket $0 – $8,700
15% Bracket $8,700 – $35,350
25% Bracket $35,350 – $85,650
28% Bracket $85,650 – $178,650
33% Bracket $178,650 – $388,350
35% Bracket over $388,350

Using the same type of structure, this is a first cut at an equitable minimum payment schedule. Note that everybody who makes as little as $100.00 per year pays 1% (something) up to the poverty level:

Student Loan Repayment Yearly Adjusted Gross
1% Bracket $100 – $11,170 (poverty line)
5% Bracket $11,170 – $40,000
10% Bracket $40,000 – $80,000
15% Bracket $80,000 – $120,000
20% Bracket $120,000 – $220,000
25% Bracket over $220,000

Of course this may be wrong. It may be too little or too much. But, it looks very fair to me. We need to ask the people in these circumstances and set the rates so undue burdens are not the rule.

This is just a first look. It all depends on a fair interest rate. If the rate or the process is not fair, then let us change it as the graduated schedule must be fair. It is designed to eventually get the loans paid off but even if it does not, nobody will go broke paying off a debt that is due. So many young people look at say, their Sallie Mae payment, and they know they can't do it so they don't.

Even if you have a 5% bogie all your life, you can live with that. I can live with that. Overall, most people do pay their loans. If it takes forever, and you can afford it, so what? You are the one that accumulated the debt in the first place. Repayment must be affordable.

If the country elects Donald Trump and he advocates the RRR bill (Explained in the book, Saving America The Trump Way! and America becomes prosperous again in many industries, then maybe just once, just once, we can have a small amnesty on student debt that is not close to 100%.

For Pete's sake we do not want the cream of the crop young people who we permitted to get saddled early with a bad life changing decision assisted by loan sharks, to not be able to work to make America the best country it can be again. I know a man with a philosophy of "Make America Great Again," feels the same.

Of course even with the repayment schedules above, in no instance would anybody have to pay more than the minimum monthly payment in their official payback schedule for their loan even if they could afford it.

As I have already discussed but it is worth a retread, I am aware that former students, who have been fortunate enough to get great jobs while their classmates have not, are not necessarily happy about taxpayers being involved in a process that lessens their classmates' burden. This is natural. I know that they think that since they have had to pay, everybody has to pay. I agree.

This is surely not a payment amnesty. This plan is merely to keep graduates with loans out of the debtor's prisons that are the only options promised by the best of the collection agencies operating on behalf of the government.

When somebody becomes a "deadbeat' in the student loan system; they have few other options than to hide from the collector. Those who paid off their loans do not know the scourge of harassment. Parents often must change their phone numbers and get unlisted numbers and ask their neighbors to not acknowledge them so they can protect their children from the incessant phone calls. In America, there must be a better way.

So, I would also set up a means for any taxpayer to donate from $1.00 up to any amount of their tax refund and have it directed towards the paying down of all student loans. I would also recommend a web site in which anybody can donate by credit card to help pay down the cumulative student loan debt for American kids trying to better themselves . Payments would be apportioned only to those whose debts are in default.

I do not believe in the free lunch. So, any program must involve the debtor, though they were only 17 or 18 at the time in which they originally messed up their lives. The program also should involve the co-signors, who never would have expected the universities to make it more difficult for their graduates to get real jobs.

The student debtor and the co-signor were both duped by the academic institutions to keep the student at the institution for four or five or even six years for an undergraduate degree, though the institution was working against the parents promoting foreign students to employers rather than Americans.

We all know that universities make a big promise about the value and the future promise of an education for a successful graduate. Yet, they have taken no responsibility when the graduate is never employed.

Before any reduced opportunity for retirement (garnishment of social security etc.) should be inflicted against the loan cosigners, the cash collectors should come after the universities for promises un-kept. My final recommendation set therefore as in Chapter 1 is a bit more controversial.

All of this money that former students have signed for or have paid and will pay over the years has already gone into the coffers of universities across the nation. Despite being the only party to whom the proceeds have been given, the universities seemingly have no skin in the loan game.

And, since the product of the universities, the students, our children have not been able to achieve the American Dream as promised by the admissions counselors, and the Financial Aid Counsellors, there should be recourse. Since such universities encourage foreign students to take jobs in the US upon graduation and they also hire foreign faculty even when Americans are available, universities are a part of the problem. The recourse should be even more obvious.

In this regard, as noted in Chapter 1, I would ask the Congress to enact legislation to make colleges and universities a part of the financial solution, providing the following:

1. Collect a fee of 5% of the university's gross revenue to 25% (similar notion to the student payback schedule with different values for gross revenue) – at least something. This is to be applied to paying down all student loans. The minimum payment would be a factor of the student default rate for the institution and the percentage of gross revenue. The exact formula will need some work.

2. Severely limit the number of foreign students admitted until the unemployment rate is 3% and cap the number permitted to obtain work visas after graduation to a smaller / reasonable number.

3. Limit the number of H-1B visas for faculty to a very small number perhaps 2% of total faculty. Today the number is unlimited and often American students in American universities are shortchanged because their teachers are not fluent in English.

4. Assure the H-1B faculty member on worker visa returns to the home country after 6 years and is not promised additional time. Employee visa holders should not be permitted to get in line for green card or citizenship if they have already been granted faculty status. This is unfair to American professors.

5. Reduce all non-University H-1B visas from 85,000 (65,000) to 10,000 until the unemployment rate goes to 3%.

These recommendations do not affect those students who are doing well and can afford to pay off their debt through the normal payment schedules. However, in as much as the Congress is encouraged to remove the ability for financial companies to loan shark any student loan debtor, this plan is designed to help us all.

Even the tax payers will be helped as the five million plus, who today have no hope will be able to begin paying at least a small percentage on their loan. Eventually they will be able to pay a higher percentage, and then hopefully, they will also be able to buy a house. The greatest advantage of all in this program is nobody will feel they are in a debtor's prison with no escape. Amen!

Chapter 4   Is it really OK that legal foreign nationals enjoy the highest paying jobs?

Should American college graduates remain unemployed?

There is a major connection between the influx of legal and illegal foreign nationals with jobs in America and college graduates coming up empty when looking for a job after graduation. Not only are American Corporations offshoring the best jobs they can, they are onshoring whatever jobs they can right here in America.

To be exact, onshoring refers to the relocation of business processes to a lower-cost location inside the national borders. Nearshoring refers to a company contracting a part of its work to an external company located across national borders within its own region. I have my own definition. When companies cannot offshore jobs to other countries, in a process that I call onshoring, they often hire illegal foreign nationals to perform the work.

My definition of onshoring is more the opposite of offshoring. It is the old adage that if the mountain will not come to Mahomet, Mahomet will goe to the mountaine. If you cannot take your factory overseas to produce goods with cheap labor because it would be too difficult to ship products back home, then you can produce products at home by bring cheap labor to your factory.

Seventy percent of college graduates have major student loan debt when they graduate and with foreign nationals working for less money for the same job, the competition to get a good job is tough. Yet, the student loan must be paid off.

Things are not so good for millennials who are recent college graduates. For example, back in 2012, when many of America's freshly graduating college students were just 19 years old, they chose to vote in droves for President Barack Obama — by an estimated margin of 60 percent to 37 percent over Republican Mitt Romney.

Then, when as members of the Class of 2015, they accepted their hard-earned diplomas and stared into the cold, hard abyss that is the real world. Things appear very bleak. How bleak?

Just 14 percent of the 2015 college seniors have gained steady, career-type jobs lined up for their lives after graduation. Thus, 86 percent of America's college grads — about five out of every six — have little in the way of career prospects for their post-campus lives.

Millennials to their own chagrin refuse to connect the dots. Nobody blames Obama but he was the one driving the big car known as the economy for the last eight years. It is how it is and simply by not blaming the guy that caused it does not make it go away.

Additionally, during the same time, hundreds of thousands of foreign nationals have been permitted to take jobs anywhere in the US as Obama chose not to enforce our immigration laws. We get the government we deserve. So who can pay their student loans? Who can get married and buy a home with such huge student debt and no job?

After border abuse comes visa abuse as a major immigration sins that affect American jobs. But, with the latter, it is all perfectly legal. One of my largest books by page counts to date is titled, Americans Need Not Apply! I finished this book in 2011. It is still very current.

Foreign work visa holders (legal aliens) are enjoying those great jobs that once were assured to the adult children of American citizens. Nobody wants to hear this but nonetheless, fifty-three percent of all Americans with a bachelor's degree under the age of 25 are either unemployed or underemployed. Forty-five percent of 2011 college graduates have already moved home with mom and dad.

Just like the most dangerous place for a baby today is in the womb, the most dangerous place for a job seeking American today is—in America—especially if you are a recent college graduate. Yet, the legal aliens that hold the jobs in America seem to be doing just fine.

All over the United States, "middle class jobs" are being replaced by "low income jobs" and young college graduates are being hurt by this transition more than almost anyone else. Massive numbers of young college graduates are now working jobs that do not even require a high school degree. Some of the statistics about young college graduates are absolutely astounding. The following is from a recent CNBC article....

In the last year, they were more likely to be employed as waiters, waitresses, bartenders and food-service helpers than as engineers, physicists, chemists and mathematicians combined (100,000 versus 90,000). There were more working in office-related jobs such as receptionist or payroll clerk than in all computer professional jobs (163,000 versus 100,000). More also were employed as cashiers, retail clerks and customer representatives than engineers (125,000 versus 80,000).

Has government stopped working for the American people? The book, Saving America: The Trump Way introduces RRR, which is a unique plan for economic recovery and job creation. This major Trump bestseller, written by yours truly, sees illegal and legal immigration as a major cause of American unemployment today. More than anything, it is the reason why former students cannot pay off their student loans. There are no jobs for them.

Yet, despite how true it is, it is not politically correct to talk about it. Hillary Clinton believes that all Americans ought to suck it up and give our jobs to whichever foreign national asks for them—even if we need to be employed. I do not think that way, nor does Donald Trump.

The book does not address porous borders or illegal / legal immigration per se. Its purpose is to demonstrate that even if we could create a lot of jobs for Americans in the private sector or public sector, it would not help Americans if the jobs were given to foreign nationals – illegal or legal.

The Trump Economic Plan acknowledges that a good part of the blame for the lack of American jobs is the lack of immigration and visa protection by our government. Washington does a lot worse than nothing.

American jobs are being taken away by the millions by foreign nationals and instead of stopping it; our government enables it. Even Mitt Romney's counter to Obama's de-facto Dream act was filled with promises for legal immigrants to get jobs in America. Mr. Romney, and Mr. Obama need to be awakened that there are few jobs today that are available and those that are available go first to foreign nationals and then to Americans. Donald Trump is for America and Americans First!

Some may argue that all the good jobs have already been offshored. It certainly is true that millions of our best jobs in all industries, white and blue collar alike, have gone overseas. This chapter is not about those jobs, though any real jobs plan must defame the negatives of offshoring, and RRR /Trump surely does that.

It clearly addresses how to fix offshoring. Foreign nationals taking American jobs, is a lot easier problem to fix because it is caused by the US government. Yet, it is not politically correct and both President Obama and Hillary Clinton show they are more interested in pandering to Latinos than assuring Americans get jobs before foreigners. Donald Trump loves Latinos but his job as he sees it is for Americans First!

If we replace those in charge of Congress, and Mr. Trump, God-willing, who is for Americans first, becomes our President, the unemployment problem caused by immigration of all kinds will go away. There is no chance of any improvement if Mrs. Clinton is elected. It will be a third Obama term of misery! Millennials can expect nothing. Meanwhile the interest keeps piling up on the student loans.

Five to ten million American jobs and perhaps even more have been taken from Americans by both legal and illegal foreign nationals. The jobs are gone for the same reason they are gone when companies offshore good American jobs. Using foreign nationals in America is the moral equivalent of offshoring jobs. In both cases, non-Americans are working and Americans are unemployed. Trump will end this and American student graduates will be getting the best jobs in America.

Companies always seek cheap labor. Those companies that cannot take jobs offshore, such as housekeeping, construction, meatpacking, etc., do the next best thing for their bottom line. They hire work visa carrying legal foreign nationals as well as illegal foreign nationals to lower their overall wages. For Americans, it is no different than offshoring in its effect.

A foreigner has taken an American job in America instead of overseas. Life becomes a bit better for the foreigner overnight, while it does irreparable harm to the American victim of job theft.

The Republicans elites and the establishment guys like Bush and McCain do love cheap labor, while conservatives like Americans to have the jobs. American employees working for a fair wage is the American way.

Why the progressive liberals, who belong to the Democrat Party keep voting for cheap labor is a mystery to me. Somebody should tell them they are after the same cheap labor that the establishment elite Republicans seek.

Liberal progressives whine about the rights of the poor and the underserved in America, yet, they create more poor people and more underserved people by advocating for amnesty, which is a sin against America and all Americans.

I regret that it seems that Democrats would love to forego charity for the poor for a vote for the Democratic Party. Only in this scenario does blind loyalty to Obama and Hillary amnesty make any sense. A vote for a Democrat, despite the negative effects on a human being, would be the only rationale for supporting a policy that hurts people. Is the Democratic Party worth all the carnage it creates?

Surely, many American jobs are still in America but they are no longer held by American employees. That is because American companies have a penchant for cheap labor. To read other opinion pieces of mine on illegal foreign nationals, please type the following titles into your browser: "Enforce immigration laws: quickest way to create good jobs for Americans!" or "Forget about the immigration EASY button; hit the immigration stop button.

Both articles are found on the Internet and were once published on America's finest conservative blogosphere.

Legal Immigration

If there is nothing wrong with legal immigration, whether it is from work visas or from green cards, or from foreign students taking the seats in the best American universities, then perhaps real Americans should just sit back and remain unemployed?

Despite the pandering to the Latino community in particular, though not all jobs are taken by Latinos, excessive work visas hurt Americans in the workplace.

Since companies use legal foreign nationals to drive down wages, it does not help the country overall? Ask yourself, do legal immigrants—those with a work visa, not a visa that leads to citizenship, contribute to American unemployment? The answer of course is YES of course. When Americans are out of work, the last thing that is necessary for Americans is more "other" people, who are not American, to do the work. Recent college graduates, though perhaps never employed because of foreign nationals are out of work. They are not in the queue waiting for jobs to come open.

Long before thinking about becoming citizens legally via a work visa as opposed to an immigration visa, foreign nationals out-negotiate Americans for jobs in this country using a low wage demand as their favorite bargaining chip. Several million a year are admitted into the US, and they take the best American jobs. Some years more legal aliens are permitted in the US than those that come illegally.

And, so American university graduates with no jobs cannot pay back their student debt—even though they would love to do so.

Many Americans who think we do not do enough for immigrants do not know that each year more aliens come legally into the US than the total of all other countries in the world combined. If you do not believe that, check my facts!

Those who come legally are guaranteed a job, as part of their work visa or they must go home. Rest assured, they almost never go home. American lawyers assure their never departure date. Instead, concerned only of their own well-being, they take your job or your children's jobs! They are the biggest reason why recent American college graduates cannot find jobs. They offer no apologies.

After a number of years because the line to citizenship is so long and there are many line-jumpers that delay their acceptance, eventually those that do it the right way get the call and they become citizens. After many years of waiting, with the last years holding permanent residency in the US with a green card, they go through initiation and they learn about America as they become citizens. These are not the legal aliens of which I speak.

About 1.5 million per year promise not to seek citizenship. Instead, they get a work visa or student visa. They pop in legally and take slots in our best schools and then take our best jobs when they graduate. To come to America on a legal work visa, these foreign nationals must promise to go home. But, they do not go home, and our weak government does not demand it.

Our government lies to those who come the right way and they lie to Americans and they make Americans feel guilty for not giving up our country to foreigners. Our government permits lawyers, ostensibly their cronies, to override the intention of the visa holder by changing it miraculously into a green card application for permanent residence.

Americans do not approve of this distortion as it hurts the sincere immigrant and favors the opportunist, who fraudulently and legally takes our children's highest paying job opportunities.

These are the ones that hurt Americans because they must hold jobs in order to gain the green card status from their former non-immigration type visa. Why would a government that favors its own citizens permit this? The only answer I have is that our government no longer represents the people.

Our government decides to listen to their story and place them ahead of the line for permanent residency. Immigration lawyers make tons of money in this process. This chicanery is so outrageous and the numbers are so large that it hurts America and it hurts Americans.

Americans would love to have the jobs these foreign nationals are given simply because Congress permits them to work for a pittance and American firms are happy to hire them for a pittance. They are not at all dummies. They are bright indeed, and they do well in the American workplace. These legal migrants are the major cause that wages in this country are going down, while inflation is going up. Don't expect American corporations, benefitting from the lower wages to complain.

It would be wrong for the RRR / Trump plan to ignore this type of line jumping even though the line jumpers are legal. This is a trick by major corporations and academic institutions to exercise greed and increase their bottom lines.

It may help them but this practice continues to have a devastating effect on the ability of American citizens to gain and hold the best jobs in America. Without jobs, college graduates cannot pay down their student loans.

Do colleges and universities do the right thing?

For a long time, I have been unhappy about the way most American colleges and universities conduct business with impunity, offering no student guarantees at all. They leave students with huge debts from loans and they give them inadequate non-unique skills to fight for a job position in this economy.

Perhaps even worse, they over-admit foreign students, often with preferential treatment to compete with their own American graduates. In some institutions, foreigners are given admission before Americans to help the university reach its "diversity quota."

Moreover, for the sake of "diversity," Universities have developed a penchant to hire foreigners to teach American students. They have no problem firing American citizens as faculty or staff to make room for those visa holders who will work for less money to teach at the institution.

Many foreign national faculty members have a very difficult time with the English language and this hurts the prospects of a better education for American students. Yet, the financial deal of getting a fully qualified foreign national PhD for peanuts is so good that universities are thrilled to bring them on as low-level, low-cost faculty members, even if the students do not learn as well.

As a retired Assistant Professor from a Pennsylvania University, I cannot understand why anybody with a child in college or graduate school would not be upset that the only winners in the academic game today are the colleges or universities and the loan sharks who benefit from the usury level interest on student loans.

After commencement, three quarters of the student graduates flounder for many years trying to pay back the huge debt for an education that has not helped their lives. Recently I have read stories of student debt getting paid off so late in life that the government has had to begin garnishing social security wages.

Today, the bottom line is that a college degree does not provide the lifetime assurances that it once did. Legal foreign nationals have seen to that. Yet, somehow the universities have no culpability, even though they are the only ones collecting clean cash on the deal. Universities have no regrets when they have an assured income.

American college-graduates, in increasing numbers, are not being employed in their chosen profession if at all, and they are coming home in droves to live. When parents go looking for reasons why their children are not doing well after college, they must look everywhere. The first place I would look is at the university's programs and the credentials of its faculty. What promises were made to students to get them to enroll as freshmen? What was delivered?

Most Americans feel when their child is unemployed after a number of years after graduation, that there is something wrong with the kid. That's why our government, lending institutions, and academic institutions get away with their charade. In many cases, an expensive university education is not the best thing for a high school graduate whose parents are not of means.

More and more parents of children with debt, stuck with cosigning obligations, are beginning to talk to each other. They have taken notice to the huge student loan debt ($1.3 Trillion overall) for such little job opportunity. Meanwhile, universities are continuing to increase their tuition and enrollment numbers, while there are no jobs for anybody but foreign graduates, who agree to work well below the normal wage.

Ironically, graduate school enrollments in universities are up because recent college graduates cannot get jobs. The new graduate that cannot find work elects to go even deeper in debt thinking they will be better prepared to get a good job with a Master's Degree. It is another charade.

When American students come out of graduate school, they often find a foreign national graduate with an MS or an MBA from the same university competing to take away their job opportunities. Since the legal foreign nationals work for less, they are hired before Americans. It is the new America.

Parents should demand to see the university profiles to know what percentage of the students are American and what percentage are on student visas (foreign nationals). Parents should demand that universities stop granting admission to so many foreign students and they should demand that they hire Americans professors first for university teaching positions.

Parents should get some level of guarantee that if their children attain such and such grades, they should expect to get a job upon graduation in their field of study. After parents spend all that money on a "quality" education, there is nothing to show when the child is unemployed.

Only when universities are accountable for student graduate failures, things will improve in academia, but not until. Less foreign student admissions and less foreign professors is a good start.

Do legal aliens take jobs?

If I told you that anywhere from 1 million to 2.5 million foreigners per year take the great jobs for which your children as university students, have long prepared, you would be irate. Be irate then! You should know that our Congress and our President do not care how irate you become and their agnostic look at your problem continues to make the problem worse, not better. Meanwhile, while they permit even more and more work visas to take more and more jobs from American college graduates.

On June 15, 2012, President Obama showed his disdain for jobless Americans by unilaterally implementing a de facto "Dream Act." This unprecedented unconstitutional action thumbs a nose at hard working Americans and their college graduate children who cannot find jobs in the United States.

It protects at least 800,000, and up to 2 million illegal foreign nationals from deportation. For a jobless, America, it adds insult to injury as it also grants them work permits, thereby adding millions of new job competitors to an already strained USA labor force.

The US government and President Obama specifically, in this instance have proven that they no longer care about American citizens.

Having a work visa, most notably the H-1B white collar type assures that legal foreign nationals will get jobs before Americans. The typical ways that legal aliens get into the US are via the following:

1. Legal permanent resident program, known as the green card
2. Student visas
3. Student work visas
4. H-1B white collar visas

The H-1B visa is known for snatching the best jobs for which your children have prepared. In addition to those listed above, there are many other legal visas that enable foreign nationals to be in America and many permit them to work in America. Technically, they do not have a right to apply for citizenship but smart lawyers advise them around the weak constraints that are inherent in the visa system.

Reading government visa documentation gives the impression that the government is doing all it can to take American jobs from Americans. In practice, it is what we find. Our Congress is very generous to foreigners by statute and by regulations with our jobs and our children's jobs. They are not as generous with solutions when their foreign favorites take your kids' jobs.

As an aside that makes matters worse, 45% of illegal aliens did not jump the border. They simply stayed in America, where they remain today. In these times of few jobs and low wages for the jobs that now exist, the blame rests squarely on the backs of foreign nationals who will do anything to work in America. Americans, of course have no such rights in their home countries. We know what Donald Trump's plans are for illegal foreign nationals even if they have graduate degrees. Then finally graduates will be able to pay off their huge loan debt.

Foreigners in the work place are taking American jobs that Americans can no longer get. Americans are second choice for jobs in America. Entry job loss is caused by illegal foreign nationals taking unskilled, low-paying jobs while Professional job loss is caused by legal foreign nationals on visas taking highly skilled, high paying formerly American jobs. It is a big problem and the title of the book says it all, and quite correctly.

It is a huge and growing problem and our government is not motivated to solve it. In fact, if you listen to any of the news outlets, when the President issued his June 15 amnesty proclamation favoring illegal workers, it was not discussed as an important issue. Why do we not hear of it? It is not politically correct that your son or daughter cannot get a job. Is it perfectly OK in this politically correct system.

On top of the fact that many Americans are put out of work by legal aliens, there is one additional issue that makes it even worse. Foreigners are sponsored by US companies until they get their green cards or until they become citizens or until they go home—often six or more years after getting your kid's job! Often, they never go home.

A recent statistic says 45% never go home. Once sponsored and hired, the legal alien is in many ways a slave to the corporation for which they work. However, it is clearly worse for them if they are not sponsored and hired. Therefore, they agree to work for substantially less wages than Americans.

In other words, the foreigners are not really winners and surely the American student graduates who are unemployed are not winners at all. So, if you or your child has been victimized by this unequal treatment of Americans v foreign nationals, make sure your representative knows it is time to make this right. Only employers and the universities are the big winners.

If a foreign worker sees that Americans are being hurt by their behavior, and they decide that it is best to come clean and admit that they gained their jobs by agreeing to work for less wages, their American sponsor will simply release them and they will be deported.

They have no rights and so they mostly stay quiet. Yes, they are treated as slaves and just as illegal foreign nationals. The system is only fair for the employer. In spite of the wishy-washy requirement that H-1B workers be paid the prevailing wage, H-1B workers and other visa workers almost always earn significantly less than their American counterparts. For example, at Intel, engineers with H-1Bs are reported to be hired for 60% of the prevailing wage in the same state.

I have worked with executive visa-holders who were doing the same job as another employee but receiving ½ or less salary. I learned that they feel indebted to the companies for hiring them and giving them a shot at America.

But, more importantly, they know that if they are not the hardest worker on the team or they create any issue at all for their employer, they will be forced to leave the US. Their business sponsor basically owns them and if the sponsor rejects them, it is almost always over and their legal hiatus ends.

Don't you think if I know all this, and now you know now it, that our Congress and President know it also? So, why is it that the system is not rigged by the government for the American employee instead of the foreign national?

Ask your representative. Ask the President. If US employers abuse the privilege of hiring visa employees, they should be the ones who suffer, not the foreign employee who knows that life is somehow not right! Surely Americans should not be the ones suffering, but nonetheless we are the ones feeling the most pain.

The legal foreigner with a visa gets hired however, not because they are more handsome or more congenial or smarter than Americans. They want a better life so much they will temporarily work for cheap wages and they will do anything not to get sent back home. American workers have been schooled to expect certain working conditions.

Foreign workers expect nothing. American businesses would love to legally put this sign outside their shops: "Americans need not apply!"

Reducing Immigration, legal and illegal, is a big answer to the jobs issue in America, but it is not the only answer. One way to assure that both illegal and legal immigration can be controlled is to replace members of the Senate and the House who do not answer your immigration questions properly. Don't forget the President's job killing amnesty.

Let's put in people like Donald Trump, who are concerned about America and Americans and who would represent Americans first. Our President has consistently shown that American citizens do not count as he chooses not to enforce US immigration laws, when it is clearly his job. Ask your representatives their posture on illegal and legal immigrants taking American jobs. You might be very surprised. Then in November, vote accordingly.

Limiting or stopping immigration completely during periods of recession is a good jobs solution for unemployed

Americans. Legal foreign nationals taking the best American jobs is a problem that was created by this elected government and it is a problem that can be fixed only by un-electing them, and finding representatives to do the will of the people. If somebody with a graduate degree is going to be called upon to flip the burgers in America, it should be one of the millions of foreign nationals who now hold America's best jobs, but only if an American does not want the job. As Americans, we, and our children deserve much better than what we receive from our government. Since our government is founded as being of the people, for the people, and by the people, country is of the, we can change this scenario and any other, anytime we please.

Chapter 5 How to Prevent More Massive Student Debt -- Intuitive

Solve Both Big Issues!

There are two big issues with the massive student debt issue as follows:

1. How to prevent students from accumulating huge student loan debts in the future.
2. How to deal with the $1.3 trillion student debt already accumulated.

This chapter and the next deal with item # 1. There are a number of clever approaches being discussed in academic and government circles regarding both of these issues.

My university wrote me a letter

On the student side, Indiana State University is ahead of the curve with the most sensible notion yet on student debt.   It is documented that 53% of students who are attending college have no idea they are accumulating a massive loan debt and that they will be asked to pay it down immediately upon graduation or dropping out of school. In the flurry of getting admitted to a favorite university, how the bill gets paid is often the last thing discussed if discussed at all.

Mom and dad and junior and missy are lulled by the hype of the notion of attending college at their choice of universities. They fill out all their forms as everybody else and the admissions department and financial aid department make a determination how much they can afford out of pocket and how much has to come in the form of various grants and aid packages including loans of various kinds.

The university tuition is always set high especially today with so many sources of funding for students. Giving a little aid to a student is no big deal today. It helps to remember the result of such a system places 70% of students who graduate in a debtor position with tens of thousands of dollars of student loans due.

When the package comes to the student along with an acceptance letter, there is euphoria on the part of the parents and the student. Johnnie and Janie are able to attend a great college and whatever the loon amount is as past of the package is simply another part of the yes vote when the student signs for the package with mom and dad's permission and the student begins to matriculate the following fall semester. There appears to be no downside until the debt is due.

Indiana has decided to be a lot more honest with its students and its new student loans are down by almost 20% while the number of students accepting admission is about the same. How is it that Indiana's students do not need as much funding as those students in other universities? It's simple. Indiana tells them they are going into debt and to think carefully about the amount of debt they are about to take on as the debt from the loan will have to be paid back... and it will affect their lives after graduation.

Those looking at the Indiana program and finding it to make a lot of common-sense are suggesting the notion be more widespread than just one university in the nation. Based on Indiana's success, more schools are getting on the bandwagon.

Many are suggesting that the letters should be sent to high school students well before the prospective student chooses whether to go to college or focus on vocational training. It's like telling the whole story and not giving universities and loan sharks the edge.

Then these vigilantes against massive student debt suggest that each college should administer a short quiz to incoming freshmen, to make sure they understand the kind of debt they are about to assume.

The tests in many ways would help to insulate colleges against nuisance lawsuits later, when students can't find jobs and they blame their college administrators for not disclosing the full extent of their debt. But, more than vindicating the institutions of higher learning, the idea is to provide an honest wakeup call that hits the student and parents between the eyes that success is not a sure thing but the debt that will be accumulated is a sure thing.

Intuitive solution not on the US table

Why is it that if you and I now know and those in charge know that the system stiff our young? Americans should have been informed years ago that the system was rigged to punish kids for trying to succeed. Millennials, the kids who are most affected by the student loan rigged system, do not get it and will vote for the same people who created their dilemma to be able to create more pain for other young people.

Donald Trump hates rigged systems. He got his wealth from a financial bump from dad when young and then he had to work hard to become successful. This student debt system creates kids whose options have become a life from 23 to 65 years of age in a debtor's prison with a huge loan preceded by a great four or five year stint of raucous parties and an enjoyable life on campus at a great college with perhaps even in an eventual degree, not good enough for a job—or saying no to all that and taking one bite at a time.

Colleges and universities and even parents package the deal so sweetly so that the new high school seniors—junior sirs or misses—cannot say no. After the four or five year great time post high school, their life is over and they are placed into the bucket with all of the other 70% who are responsible for the $1.3 Trillion of student loan borrowing in America.

Sorry, there is no escape once a high school student elects to take the plunge into the student debt pool. Congress saw to that. Congress decided that there is no way out of student debt and there is no way to make the pain any less severe than having the young in America to believe their lives are being spent in a debtor's prison. Meanwhile the same Congress has tricks so that those related to them in their work effort can escape without owing anything. No Virginia, life is not fair unless you are a Congressman.

So, is there an intuitive solution to high school students unknowingly signing up for a life of bondage devised intentionally so that a prestigious university can collect cold hard cash from the unknowing debtors and deliver little if anything? A job! Sorry! Universities get jobs for foreign nationals not white privileged Americans.

Yes, there is an intuitive solution but millennials I fear would not get it. I can recall that when I went to college and worked with the janitorial staff to get my tuition paid, the head janitor had a sign outside his office. It read "A college education is a four year loaf on dad's brad, and the college comes out fresh with a lot of crust."

I understood the truth there but I was working my way through along with a few affordable loans and an academic scholarship. Yet, I understood as these gentleman on the janitorial staff knew that there were a lot of bold and brazen contemporaries of mine who were convinced that they knew everything and what was given to them was well deserved. I had met them. I felt they were smarter than I until the first tests started coming back and then I knew they were made of wind.

I have three millennial children and like Donald Trump's brood, my kids appreciate everything they get. I thank God for that. They tell me that their peers respect little about the old America and do not care about America as their parents do. They have not experienced America as I know it or my children know it.

I regret that for them as America is such a wonderful place compared to all others. I wish millennials were not forced to listen to the labored breathing of coffee-breathed liberal progressive professors in ultra-Marxist universities. As a professor myself, I know these people and I understand why our young in America are so distraught about America. Yet, there is no rational explanation other than the fraud perpetrated on all Americans by the elite academicians whose disdain for rugged individualism or the freedom to be an individual has affected the most gentle minds in America—the youth. Millennials! Many young parents say that the first time they realized how smart their parents were was when they had their own children.

Unfortunately, the current world brought to us by Obama and the Clintons, a world full of student debt with no escape... with foreigners holding all the respectable jobs in America, and our smartest college graduates sunken in massive debt, the millennials have been convinced by their professors that the reason they can never enjoy a family, a home, a fine job, and hope for the future is because America sucks. As a professor and as a guy who knows these liars, I am so sorry that students in their charge, millennials as we call them, have fallen for this bullshit.

The fact is that America is the best place to be unless you want somebody else to control your life.

So what does this have to do with how intuitive it is to solve the problem of more students taking on massive debt when they do not have to do so? I regret to say that even my children agree that most millennials would not accept a solution to anything that permits America to look good in the final act...even if that solution permitted them to escape the huge debt and be able to buy a home and start a family. Academicians who are often reprobates in society have convinced many of our children they are better off sucking it up for the cause rather than trying to better themselves.

Would the millennials at a high school age accept the notion that taking on a huge student debt may be unhealthy for them later in life? Well, it all depends on when an obstinate youth becomes a millennial and whether they will ever accept the truth under any circumstance. Millennials are so wrapped up in Hillary Clinton today that it is obvious the truth has no meaning in their lives

Worse than that! Some millennials have escaped joblessness and debtors prisons. Many of these escapees have become teachers of our children. What does this mean? It means that if I were to suggest and I am going to suggest that we conduct formal education for ninth graders and senior high students about the risks of not being successful enough to pay off student debt, there would be some "smart" teacher would show themselves off as the primo example of how I am wrong.

They would devote inestimable energy to convince the millennial to sign up for an unbearable amount of debt so that they too could be as smart as Mr. or Miss Larson. Since the people own the schools and the people elect the schoolboards, the people must now more than ever make sure ideological teachers in high school do not harm the future of our children.

So, what is the solution? We must rely on our "honest" government to get the right message out as early as possible about the risks of huge debt and no prospects for a life. When our government is dishonest, we must replace it at the tip with people like Donald Trump.

Not every teacher and not every government employee and not every politician is against the people but it sure seems most are. We must demand that our children learn that a college education may very well cost a student a better life if it is not planned and accepted properly. The sooner the better.

College must no longer be the default for all high school students and all the other choices need to be explored by students as they once had been. Kuder tests and other vocational tests need to be brought back and implemented. White collar professionals should help form white collar potential career paths and blue collar professionals should present the same for the trades and the physical work place.

In terms of making sure we do not add more bad debt to the $1.3 Trillion currently owed, we need to make sure that each of those who might accept debt for a larger opportunity, do so with their eyes wide open and with the facts all known.

I have two last suggestions for the period in which all the college signings are done by the high school student.

1. Online course
2. Preprinted complete information forms

1. Each student who plans to attend college should be required to complete an online course of study in his or her junior or senior year in which they learn about all the specifics about the opportunities of a college degree. The material should include the risks of debt and other methods of paying for tuition, room, board, & books.

2. In addition to the letters and the courses and the brochures that explain to high school students the potential for devastating lifelong debt, the state and national governments should add a student debt information form that is as formal as all the other federal and state and lender / borrower forms.

It should be prefilled based on the student database, with specific information about the borrower. Based on the borrower's high school record and the track record of success for the chosen institution, a computer model should produce a probability of success, calculated based on past histories. Additionally, all the anticipated costs and the anticipated payback period and amounts should be preprinted along with anything else that would be helpful to the student making an informed decision about debt. This should be regardless of its impact on the university.

Chapter 6 How to Prevent More Massive Student Debt – Income share agreements.

What is an income share agreement?

An Income Share Agreement (or "ISA") is a financial vehicle in which an individual or organization gives a fixed amount of money to a recipient who, in exchange, agrees to pay back a percentage of his/her income for a fixed number of years. It is not debt per se, and unlike a student loan liabilities incurred in such an agreement go away in the event of student bankruptcy.

For a high school student, it is a better option in many ways than dealing with loans sharks but care must be taken that ISA sharks are not permitted into student programs.

With $1.3 Trillion and counting as the massive debt accumulated by students. Many parents of high school students are rethinking college as the only vehicle for future success. The fact is that those who know best—alumni are changing their opinions as time goes by. For example, studies show that only half of alumni 'strongly agree' their college degree was worth the cost.

Student loan debt is so huge it is convincing graduates to put off buying homes and cars and having children, and the increasing flow of federal money as loans won't fix the problem. It actually makes the system less sustainable.

The House and the Senate have been meeting on this matter and this was the message they heard when higher-education experts gave testimony to a recent congressional committee hearing on financing higher education. The major alternative to traditional loans was placed on the table at the session. It is what we have described as income-share agreements (ISAs).

With an ISA, students pay a fixed percentage of their future income to investors who finance their educations. This idea intrigued both Democratic and Republican members of this joint economic committee.

They prepared a bipartisan bill that would permit the development of ISAs nationwide. It is called the Investing in Student Success Act (HR-3432) and it has been sponsored by Reps. Todd Young, R-Ind., and Jared Polis, D-Colo.

Former Governor Mitch Daniels is currently the President of Purdue University and he likes the idea for a number of reasons. He was the star witness at their hearing. Purdue University President Mitch Daniels, former Republican governor of Indiana and hoped-for presidential candidate in 2012, was the star witness at the hearing.

Rep. Carolyn Maloney, D-N.Y. was a negative voice in the hearings as she simply does not buy the notion.
Private loans pose "significant risks" and will not "magically solve" student debt problems, Maloney said in a lengthy opening statement. She asked the witnesses, including Daniels to explain how ISAs would protect students from "predatory practices."

Daniels quickly pointed out the obvious that the student debt problem is "still getting worse." He cited facts such as a newly released second Gallup-Purdue Index, a survey of 60,000 college graduates that asks how debt has affected their lives.

The survey found that only half of alumni "strongly agree" their college degree was worth the cost, and that the median loan is $30,000. Loans above $25,000 are associated with "significantly" longer delays in starting grad school or businesses, the survey found. With a median loan of $30,000, that means there are loans much higher and their prospects for success are much lower. Graduate students who financed their advanced degrees with loans are saddled with debt often well over $100,000.00

Daniels did not lie down on the matter. Instead, he made a forceful defense of ISAs, emphasizing their certainty and their status as equity rather than lending: "You want debt-free education? Here it is."

ISAs could be a good replacement for the federal PLUS loans intended for graduate and professional students, as well as for private loans – existing options that Daniels said were largely to blame for the "nightmarish anecdotes" of student loan debt.

Legislation should ensure that ISAs would be "dischargeable in bankruptcy," unlike today's student loans, and exempt them from state usury laws, he said.

Purdue itself is mulling its own program for ISAs, Daniels said in his written testimony. It's reviewing "six serious proposals" from potential managers of an ISA program and expects to make a decision by the end of October.

Andrew Kelly is the director of the Center for Higher Education Reform at the American Enterprise Institute. He has a lot of stake in the game and wants the problem solved in the best way.

Kelly fired a big volley at universities who are fat cats in the scenario. He said they are " signaling its priorities" when it heavily depends on adjuncts – away from teaching and toward "amenities." In other words, the cheap out on faculty costs and try to attract students with fluff and fanfare and impressive luxuries to which they are unaccustomed.

Students are in a terrible position now because the value of a college degree is declining but "the counterfactual is worse" – having only a high-school education, Kelly said. Colleges provide "no signal to students about the value of different offerings" in terms of earnings potential, and they have wide latitude to "price discriminate" against students. The financial aid packages they put together for students are a disgrace.

Kelly would like to see Congress institute a "performance floor" to yank back federal money from those schools that have the worst student outcomes. He is also for risk-sharing so schools have "skin in the game," Kelly said. If students do not do well consistently, those schools should pay through the nose.

The ISA idea is not completely new. In fact, it is already taking hold as entrepreneurs have entered the space to create organizations that engage in the share agreements. Two such companies are Upstart and Lumni. They fund student college educations under ISAs.

To give a sense of how important this idea is for the financial health of college graduates in the future, consider that out of the approximately 38 million borrowers, with 1.3 trillion in debt load, the default rate is about 6 million. Students who default are off the lifetime opportunity charts and are heading for lives as deadbeats.

Unlike Sallie Mae and other government and quasi-government loans or private student loans, ISAs would not create any student debt that immediately starts accruing interest after graduation. Instead the ISA would entitle an investor to a small percentage of the future stream of a student's cash flows across many years following college.

The amount of cash per time period and the number of years are two variables in the ISA negotiations.

To put that in perspective, I have asked some students in default why they would not pay at least something towards their loans. Several have told me that when things were tough right after school, they got mom and dad to pay a forbearance which kept them out of default and the bill collectors. However, not a dime of that went towards the principal.

Once the forbearance period expired, the debt was higher and the payments had no bearing on income. Students who tried to pay and eventually defaulted became disillusioned at the significant interest rates and the minimum payments required. In many cases it was either default or starve. This cannot happen in the ISA plan if it is structured properly and the lobbyists do not make it another cash cow for government and financial institutions.

Chapter 7 Reminder of the Cost of an undergraduate degree

The plight of the poor rich

Before I take you to the SLA Counterpoint in Chapter 8, as copied word for word from a great article, I want to offer a few thoughts. The first of my unnumbered thoughts is that rich people own the world. There is no question about it. No argument will change that fact. Theoretically, if they wanted to, they could simply eliminate the rest of us. That surely would not be fair but they could do it as they own all the major resources, the armies, and the armaments.

We could probably throw in for good measure that they own the leadership in most if not all countries. More than likely, the only things that keeps them from taking over everything is #1, they do not trust the other rich guys, and #2, there would be no services they could buy if we were not available, walking the earth, to perform them.

I am not rich but I think I have made it to someplace in the middle class. I have a BS and an MBA. Great rich people through taxes and through contributions to my college and to the government made it possible for me to win a half scholarship for achievement and a half-tuition loan (National Defense Student Loan) because my parents did not have enough money to send me to college. Two halves do make a complete whole in my case, but in the end, just $50.00 a year came from my private funds.

I was seventeen years old until the beginning of my second semester in college. I was tickled to pieces to be able to go to a great college. I also got a job at the school for $1.25 per hour under the Federal Work Study Program, again mostly paid for by some rich person's taxes. The college paid 10% and the federal government paid 90% of my hourly rate.

I am very happy that rich people exist, and I am glad they share their gains with regular people. I was a clear beneficiary. I do agree that the pendulum has gone too far with a tyranny of the underclass against the rich.

Today, the school I attended, whose tuition way back in time was $950 per year with no special fees other than graduation, is now $34,720 per year. That figure includes fees for all kinds of activities. Those amenities all cost money.

The full load without books estimated at $1500 per year is in the following table:

COSTS	RESIDENT	COMMUTER
Tuition and Fees (full-time)	$34,720	$34,720
Average Room and Board	$12,136	N/A
Total	$46,856	$34,720

That's well over $100,000 if you are lucky to finish in four years. A little known statistic is that only 1% of the students pay the full amount. In other words, 99% receive some type of package which includes grants (not paid back) and loans (must be paid back). It is all bundled nicely so that the student merely has to say OK with his or her John Hancock to be off to college the following fall. There is no documentation that I found that discusses risks.

AWARDS	RESI-DENT	COM-MUTEr
Average Financial Aid Package	$23,472	$24,911
Average Gift (Scholarship, Grant) Aid	$17,730	$17,914

Some people see the combination of the Admissions Departments and the Financial Aid Departments of universities and colleges in much the same way as a business views its marketing department and its accounting department.

Though Admissions or Enrollment Management (a more exact term) sounds better than marketing, marketing is its job nonetheless. Its mission is to convince the best students to come to the university at the listed price with some discounts.

Let's suppose the name of this college is Student Loan University (SLU). Here are some of the words a typical high school student would find when dealing with the shrewd marketeers at SLU to entice the prospective student to go along with the "AID" package, which they receive:

When determining the cost of a college education, one should also take into consideration the value. U.S. News & World Report has ranked SLU among America's best colleges for 18 straight years and Barrons consistently considers us one of the best buys in college education. [Notice there is no guarantee that you will do well.]

Approximately 99% of all full-time students attending SLU receive financial assistance, with the average scholarship being $10,815 [that leaves 34,720-$10815 =$23,905 per year for you to pay]. We encourage every student to apply for financial aid no matter what their family circumstances are. Only after you have applied and been considered for all available assistance will you have a true idea of what your costs will be.

SLU offers a payment plan through Tuition Management Systems (TMS), which allows families to make monthly payments on the balance of tuition, fees, room and board less any financial aid received.

If the cost of the Tuition Management System seems too high for a family, it helps for students to remember that after four years of accumulated interest, the same plan for the next four years would be even more expensive. Sometimes, college tuition at the institution of choice is simply too expansive and a nice community college and / or state college combination may deliver the same benefits at substantially lower costs.

Chapter 8   ISA Student Loan Counterpoint

Point discussed; counterpoint follows

Is An ISA another way to feed the rich form the miniature coffers of the poor?

Benjamin Studebaker is into politics, economics, and international relations. He has a blog at benjaminstudebaker.com and he would love you to visit him to check out his writings. I did.

He explains himself as a guy who is making "Yet Another Attempt to Make the World a Better Place by Writing Things."

Studebaker has written what his peers might consider a controversial piece as it does not conform to what is becoming the new conventional wisdom in the lucrative "student loan industry." He titles his piece:

"How ISAs Allow Rich People to Exploit College Students" By Benjamin Studebaker

A friend of mine at Purdue University recently informed me that under the leadership of former Governor Mitch Daniels (R-IN), Purdue has become the first major American university to offer Income Sharing Agreements (ISAs) to students as a new alternative to traditional student loans. ISAs are exploitative and morally disgusting. Here's why.

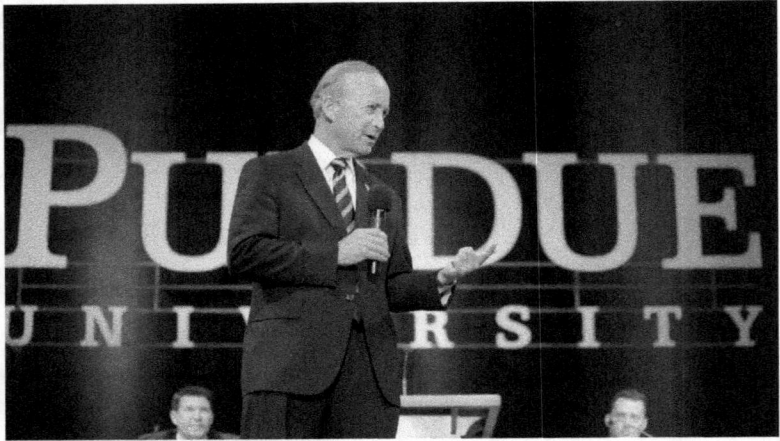

There are many different ways to pay for college around the world. Traditionally, in the United States, we have a two-tier system in which wealthy families pay for their kids to go to school out of pocket while poor and middle class families often have their kids borrow some or all of the money they need. Student loans are borrowed at relatively low interest rates, but students still end up paying back the lenders more than the full value of their tuition.

Most student loans are provided by the government, which runs most of the public universities, so in effect interest on government loans is being paid into the same public sector that runs the universities—effectively, many poor and middle income students are being charged a regressive tax for being unable to pay out of pocket.

Loans must be repaid irrespective of how much students earn after graduating, which means increasingly large numbers of underemployed college graduates have their lives significantly blighted by student debt.

Most European countries do not operate this way.

In England, students repay student loans only if their incomes exceed about $30,000. If there is any debt remaining 30 years after the loan is taken out, the debt is waived. But interest is still charged on the loans, so students that borrow can still end up paying more than students whose parents pay out of pocket.

In Germany, student fees are negligible and most German university funding comes out of general taxation, with external grants making up most of the remainder. This is the kind of funding scheme Bernie Sanders pushes for.

Another option is the graduate tax, which was proposed in the UK but ultimately rejected. A graduate tax allows the state to charge a flat income tax on all college graduates. Compared to the income tax, a flat graduate tax is regressive and if the rate is high enough it enables the state to charge far more money for college than the present tuition system.

It's even cruel to young rich people, who could end up paying exorbitant amounts of money for college if their earnings are high enough. That said, a graduate tax is more progressive than a flat fee, and in that respect it might be marginally better than the way Americans currently do things.

But ISAs are completely indefensible. There is nothing good about them at all and they are without a doubt the least ethical way to fund a university system. Here's how they work:

Private investors lend students money and in exchange, the student promises to pay the private investors a fixed percentage of their income for a fixed number of years no matter what their future income might be.

It doesn't sound so bad when you don't think very hard about it, but the negative consequences of ISAs are many and severe:

Private sector investors don't have any reason to lend a student money unless they believe they can make a profit off that student. This means that students in degrees that aren't associated with high-paying jobs will become more difficult to fund the more dominant ISAs become.

The more dominant ISAs become and the fewer financial alternatives students have to ISAs, the weaker the students' negotiating position becomes and the easier it is for private investors to extract the maximum return.

As with interest on student debt, because affluent families pay out of pocket, ISAs are a regressive tax on coming from a poor or middle class family. But student debt is mostly repaid to the state, and the state uses that money to fund many public services, from the university system to welfare to infrastructure. With ISAs, the surplus extracted from students is paid to wealthy investors, directly redistributing wealth from the bottom and middle to the top of the distribution. This is extremely and nakedly regressive.

As with the graduate tax, an ISA allows the lender to potentially extract exorbitant amounts of money from graduates who quickly begin earning large incomes. But unlike the graduate tax, where the money is paid to the state, ISAs send this money directly to wealthy private investors, which is again extremely and nakedly regressive.

We have a student debt bubble, but unlike the housing bubble most student debt is owed to the government rather than private investors, and this limits the student debt bubble's ability to damage the rest of the economy. ISAs could change that. Down the road, ISAs could be packaged by Wall Street into derivatives in much the same way that mortgages were in the years leading up to the 2008 financial crisis.

ISAs in highly profitable majors like Engineering or Computer Science could be used to conceal large numbers of junk ISAs on students with low performing majors, encouraging the proliferation of subprime ISAs. Insurance could be sold on them in the same way that insurance was sold on mortgages. Eventually ISAs could become the foundations of a sequel to The Big Short, with utterly devastating consequences.

ISAs are a form of restricted indentured servitude (in which a person agrees to work for another person for a fixed amount of time in exchange for something). They are not dissimilar to outright serfdom (in which a person works some percentage of the time for themselves and some percentage of the time for a private lord).

These kinds of economic arrangements are not capitalism–they're feudalism. Under capitalism, the worker owns his own labor power–the only entity that can confiscate his wages is the state. Under capitalism, employers may not always pay fair wages to their workers, but they are never entitled to confiscate a fixed percentage of the wages of workers they do not even employ themselves.

It is not legal in capitalist societies to make someone a serf or an indentured servant. This potentially turns venture capitalists into feudal lords.

It's easy to dismiss how potentially horrifying this is–initially, ISAs may only be one of many funding options at a handful of universities. Supporters will say that you don't have to get one if you don't want one. But this is precisely how you create a class of serfs or indentured servants over time–you start by contracting small numbers of them on what looks like a voluntary basis, and you gradually expand the program, making it harder and harder for people to remain outside of it. As the alternatives become more limited, the students' negotiating power decreases further, and the investors slowly lobby the state to allow them to gradually extract higher percentages for longer periods.

Defunct presidential candidate Marco Rubio was a big proponent of ISAs–in his 2014 bill, he proposed ISAs of up to 15% of income for 30 years. Thankfully, this bill went nowhere, but it illustrates something very important–Republicans are already prepared to accept ISAs as high as 15% for as long as 30 years.

Imagine a society in which this kind of agreement has become the norm. Imagine how high the percentages might creep, how much longer the agreements might potentially become. Imagine what happens when a single wealthy investor begins accruing large numbers of ISAs. A single rich person could own 10 ISAs from 10 students at 10% and effectively own the entire labor power of a single person for 30 years. There would be nothing illegal about that under Rubio's proposal.

People think that Rubio is a moderate. What would Ted Cruz do? What would Ted Cruz do if he were elected in a political climate where these ISAs are standard practice and no longer considered controversial?

The ISA poses a clear and present danger to the freedom of the next generation of workers.
In the letter Purdue sent out to students, they totally whitewashed the program:

Purdue claims that ISAs aren't intended to replace government loans, but their intentions are no guarantee against decisions by future governments to expand the program.

Purdue claims that the ISAs they're approving will only require repayment for nine years, but what's to stop future universities and investors from demanding longer repayment as ISAs become normalized?

If Marco Rubio is cool with 15% 30 years from now, what might ISAs look like in 2040?

Purdue speaks of the ISAs' no principal balance and no interest as if these were advantages, but this conceals the real consequences–investors have no reason to agree to ISAs unless they expect to recover more than the tuition (which would be the principal if this were a conventional loan) and the amount they extract above the value of the tuition can far exceed the value of the interest payments required by conventional loans.

By "adjust with the students' income" Purdue really means "allow the investor to potentially make of a profit of thousands, tens of thousands, or hundreds of thousands of dollars from a single student".

Purdue highlights that students will pay less than expected, but this is only the case if the private investor lends foolishly and it makes no mention of the possibility that the student will pay far more than expected, which is precisely what investors are betting will happen when they make the agreement.

As time goes on, we will likely see more people using manipulative and deceptive sales tactics to foist ISAs upon unsuspecting parents and students along with accomplice politicians hawking ISAs as a policy solution to the student debt bubble. The reality is that ISAs are likely to increase the wider economic system's exposure to the risks of a burst bubble.

They are a sick ploy by rich investors to profiteer and exploit the young people of this country, potentially turning large numbers of them into serfs and exposing our economy to unreasonable systemic risks. They are completely malignant with no redeeming features and every thinking person should reject them as such.

Thank you Mr. Studebaker

Billy Joel says it well when love is the issue. It's just a matter of trust." Studebaker is right because as we have learned in the Obama years, we cannot trust the government.

That is why an ISA may work and may not work. If a corrupt tyrannical government wants to control all aspects of the population, a poor ISA implementation can assure that the brightest minds from the poorest families never have an opportunity for major advancement and thus, a great living. Government will snatch it all. Yet, women marry men they trust. Men marry women they trust. Constituents vote mostly for people they trust. I trust Donald Trump implicitly. If he is lying, there is no reason to expect anything from anyone ever. I trust Trump.

Mr. Studebaker feels like I felt in the Obama years. If you got it Obama wants it. If you don't got it, you can be his friend. He will take from those who got it and give it to you 'til the end. That is simply not fair.

When honest men are revered and dishonest men are reviled, we will begin to make our turn for the better. I hope it is tomorrow!

How about this to end this chapter with a pick-me-up:

Tomorrow (Annie's Song) Lyrics

The sun'll come out
Tomorrow
Bet your bottom dollar
That tomorrow
There'll be sun!

Just thinking about
Tomorrow

Clears away the cobwebs
And the sorrow
'Til there's none!

When I'm stuck in a day
That's gray and lonely
I just stick out my chin
And grin, and say--

The sun'll come out
Tomorrow
So ya gotta hang on 'Til tomorrow
Come what may
Tomorrow! Tomorrow! I love ya, tomorrow
You're always a day away

Chorus

Tomorrow! Tomorrow! I love ya, tomorrow
You're always a day away!

Summing it up

The pros say that if the market for ISAs takes off, "you'll see a spectrum" of offerings. Mitch Daniels agrees. Even students who don't get the best terms, according to Daniels will have "some limits" on how much they must repay. Investors will likely bid higher for students in degrees and career paths they think are the strongest in the market, he said. Today we trust in a student loan system that really stiffs the little guy. Though ISA's may be as bad as Studebaker points out, if somebody we trust puts up a few guarantees, maybe it can be a solution. Most Americans at this time trust Donald Trump.

Daniels suggests that the most frequent use of ISAs would probably be to "recapitalize a student" after a couple years in school. Alumni and philanthropies could also fund ISAs for students who aren't the strongest economic bets, he added. I like that an awful lot if it could happen. I became reasonably successful in life because rich people decided their multi-millionth dollar was not worth as much as seeing a smile on my face. That's how I see it.

Sen. Mike Lee a Republican from Utah who does not particularly like Donald Trump, but who hopefully will come around, offered an initiative by Utah Valley University to give students guidance on financial services, and asked how much it would cost for schools to tell students the debt load per major. This is a great idea. If universities don't do it well it actually is a good thing for the government at the state level to do.

Daniels said it would cost "Approximately zero" "A little counseling, a little financial advice goes a long way," especially if families learn they don't have to borrow so much. The worst thing is for everybody who can change it to suggest that all solutions are bad and leave it the way it is.

Does my major make a difference? Yes!

We showed you the simple subtle marketing in the last chapter. How can you say no even if at the end you owe almost $100,000? The reality is that far too many individuals who have found themselves mired in student loans admit they jumped in far too quickly with little information.

Many students have borrowed more than they needed because they could. Some of it was to afford their weekly beer allotment for sure. Some tried to attain funds in the cheapest ways possible. If they had it to do over again, they would agree that funding college should really be five easy steps, in this order

- ✓ Individual and their parents
- ✓ Friends and family
- ✓ Scholarships and grants
- ✓ Federal loans
- ✓ Private loans.

Not willing to wait for any of the first four often leads a prospective student into an eventual abyss. Off course the obvious source here is to look to personal savings and what parents are willing to contribute. When my dad said he would help and I asked how much, he said, "You could live here for the next four years." I had figured I could do that anyway but maybe not…it was dad's house.

It's necessary here to decide that if a student/his or her parents do have the capital to pursue a degree, what schools are in their range? Is it worth pursuing further funding for that expensive dream school? This is obviously a question for individuals to decide. From here, one may consider friends and family – this could be anyone from wealthy siblings, to successful mentors or grandparents. Next remains the last of the 'free' money sources found in grants and scholarships. If you stop at the loan shark's office unfortunately, you will get a loan and it may be huge. It may be so huge that this whole book was written to solve problems that guys like you encounter!

Chapter 9   For-Profit Institutions

Should for profit schools even exist?

For-Profit institutions have probably funded a few scientists who created solutions for problems that are making life better across the world. Their stories are not told because so many have failed in life because they were artificially lifted to be among the gifted and they had few gifts at all from God that a college education would amplify.

So, another increasingly popular topic in the student debt debate, for-profit colleges have come under increased scrutiny in recent years. As an explanation, for-profit colleges are often exactly what they sound like – colleges run by substantial, publicly traded companies, or private equity firms, who answer to the interests of shareholders.

In search of returns, not necessarily the best shakes for the best students, these institutions recruit high numbers of students with questionable methods, and they do not always deliver on their promises. The institutional concerns towards students at these schools tend to begin and end with tuition payment, regardless of who pays the bill.

For-profit schools have made a substantial impact on federal student loan debt on the negative side of the ledger. At for-profits, 96 percent of students take out loans, and the average student ends up with $40,000 in debt. Remember there are

50% in many cases if this were a mean, who have substantially higher debt.

In addition, a 2012 study found that as the government raised federal aid amounts, for-profits closely matched these increases with surges in tuition. They knew they could get away with it as the loans were there to cover tuition. Next, one can argue parallels between for profit student loans, and subprime mortgage loans during the crisis. Neither were based on the best financial thinking available but there was a lot of greed involved.

In the Great Recession, the underwriters of subprime mortgages did not pay much attention to the creditworthiness of the loans, just as for-profits in the Student loan Industry (SLI) do not care for the creditworthiness of students when advising towards federal direct programs. Students pay big prices for being sucked in by such charlatans.

All in all, during the mortgage crisis, the government at least ruled that mortgages could not exceed the value of the home. Maybe the value of a for-profit education should have been taken into consideration during the boom of these institutions (unfortunately, calculating the value would be easier said than done).

On the bright side, increased oversight and regulation has improved the for-profit education sector in recent years. Today, the government has begun "requiring them to prove that, on average, students' loan payments amount to less than eight per cent of their annual income. Schools that fail this test four years in a row have their access to federal loans cut off, which would effectively put them out of business" So, there is a role for a lobbyist everywhere we turn.

In the past few years, the number of borrowers has decreased, and for-profit default rates have somewhat improved. The trade-off in regulation, however beneficial to the debt program overall, does have important effects on the traditional for-profit attendee. Many students at for-profits are older, part-time individuals returning to school to earn a degree.

These individuals returning to school to better themselves are obviously a huge part of the target audience of the federal loan program. Thus, if the government is going to tighten the reigns on for-profits, something must give to help these students in other respects (such as through increased funding towards community colleges or public institutions). Amen!

Potential Solutions

Now that a vast overview of the student debt market has been documented, the most significant part of this debate must be examined – solutions. By far the most frustrating part of the American political landscape today remains the constant finger pointing and grumbling without delivering viable solutions.

In all the research conducted, dozens of reporters, politicians, and journalists have proposed protests on education and student debt, but no reform. Reform is what we need but what type of reform we get depends on some honesty in government. Can we trust anybody? I trust Donald J. Trump.

You may know that at least one presidential candidate went as far as to say that when it comes to education on an international level, "We're twenty-sixth in the world. Twenty-five countries are better than us at education. And some of them are like third world countries. But we're becoming a third world country."

For the record, this cannot be even remotely verified by any valid news or research source. This candidate also offered other such groundbreaking insights on the Department of Education: "You could cut that way, way, way down". This is certainly a scintillating opinion, and as much as I would encourage all American citizen to be well informed on such complex and important issues, I would not dismiss any great ideas simply because somebody in the mainstream media suggests that I do so.

Legislative/Political Suggestions

A number of legislators, politicians, and presidential candidates have made a wide variety of suggestions. Donald Trump of course solves both the problem of $1.3 Trillion of debt as well as how to prevent its creeping increase. But Hillary Clinton and many Democrats simply take the good Trump ideas and say they are theirs.

While there are hundreds of ideas and potential fixes to the student debt problem, I would like to specifically discuss the ones that appear most valid, without attributing tem to anybody.

The ideas and proposals are from Donald Trump, Jeb Bush, Marco Rubio, Lamar Alexander, Mitch Daniels, and even a few copycats from Hillary Clinton.

To begin, there are some proposals to simplify and improve the student loan crisis. One proposes that limits be set on the federal direct loan program – allowing for a $50,000 line of credit that can be drawn upon or paid back throughout one's educational pursuit. There are few specifics on this but it clearly would reduce debt and it would force students into getting the best bang for the buck. It would also prevent regular Joe's from soiling the linens at Harvard and Princeton.

There is also a proposal that for each increment of $10,000 borrowed, students would pay back 1% of their income for 25 years. Some initiatives for improvement here involve more real world experience through internships, certifications, etc., and also through a database listing various statistics on schools to educate individuals on their decision (unemployment rates, earnings, graduation rates, and others)

Others echo this plan in some ways, saying that there should be movements in accreditation reform and income-based repayment. Marco Rubio knows the pains of student debt. After paying off his nearly $150,000 in student loans, he contends that, "People should be allowed, through internships and work study and online courses and classroom courses and life and work experience, to be able to package all of that together into the equivalent of a degree." My problem with that is who is it that grants the degree, Joe Biden?

Some Senators have advocated for making the student loan system much simpler. Through simplification of the FAFSA form that each individual must fill out for student aid, many more individuals will not be deterred by the current 108-question complex document.

Mitch Daniels is always deferred to now that he has ascended to the throne at Purdue. As noted previously, Daniels argues for the use of a more privatized system of income-share agreements, an idea championed by Nobel Prize winning economist Milton Friedman in the 1950's.

Under an income-share agreement, or ISA, students would pay for their education through a fixed percentage of their income after graduation for an allotted period of time. Typical rates are anywhere from 3 to 15 percent of income, and 5 to 20 years.

Daniels is launching his pilot junior and senior class program in the fall semester 2016. Being that Purdue has a reputation as a STEM major (science technology engineering and math) hub, many of its students would benefit from favorable rates and low percentages of income requested. Sociology majors beware.

Industry Experts

The preponderance of expert opinion says that the increasing student debt load is simply unsustainable, and policy changes must be made to help both the federal budget and the students. Next, they suggest that this change comes more from the private sector and less from the government side. Having multiple entities to share the risk of the loans – having "skin in the game" – would surely increase the quality of the loans made and their subsequent repayment.

Increased help from colleges would also be beneficial; most importantly, schools have begun to advertise better their debt and graduation statistics to let students know what to expect.

Lastly, the importance of finding out how to help those that are already ensnared by loads of debt is being pushed forward.

For those who have taken out large amounts and are stuck with no form of repayment, there must be more help in place to get these Americans back on their feet. Other than default, there are few options other than skipping the country.

The great thing about ISA's, if implemented properly, would be that if all does not work out for a student, they would not be deep in a hole of debt from which escape was not possible. Overall, there will hopefully be major changes in the future to save the student debt amount from growing rapidly larger, and from convincing students who do not belong in college to stay out or be prepared to pay the price.

From delving into the world of student debt, I know that the problem can be solved if America wants to solve it. Some have developed very complex models with many assumptions. The debt and ISA model can be adjusted based on different median incomes, costs of capital for both debt and ISA, portion of income shared, interest on the debt, etc.

Experts in the business have proposed that the United States make ISAs a more functional funding vehicle. They note that there is currently bipartisan legislation awaiting approval laying the groundwork for ISAs. They offer that the law lays out limits on time of repayment, portion of income, and states that ISAs would not be dischargeable in bankruptcy, like student debt currently. It also follows what many early adopters have already been using, by limiting repayments only to years where an individual makes $18,000 or more. Once a groundwork like this has been created, ISAs will be much easier to write up from a legal standpoint, and from a high school student perspective, they will be easier to swallow. .

If we put the Studebaker negatives aside and we find a source of trust, then by using a blend of both debt and equity – like many investments use – students would be able to pay smaller fixed payments of debt that are more manageable, while also paying an equity portion of one's salary during successful years. Thus, investors would be able to hedge some risk and receive above average returns in the most successful students. If investors make a killing, government must step in and limit the student's loss.

One would argue that the government should develop a "one size fits all" type of ISA agreement or debt/equity blend, and private companies develop their own more competitive ISAs or blends. Through the private versions, students would be able to receive more favorable rates based on thorough credit analysis looking at the individual's history, proposed university, major, and other significant factors.

This would encourage individuals to choose better, more affordable schools, and in turn encourage schools to improve their graduation and debt rates. In addition, through this system, losses can be diversified away due to the law of large numbers: with a pool of students large enough, losses from those that are not as successful can be made up for by the higher performing individuals.

Most importantly though, students who are less successful would no longer be burdened until death with large amounts of debt which in some cases goes to their cosigners. In turn, individuals would no longer have student debt hanging over their heads, and would be free to pursue whatever career path they please regardless of future earnings potential. They might even be able to buy a house.

Don't you think that the current poorer performing colleges should be required to better analyze and advertise their graduation rates, earnings potential by major, and student debt statistics? They cannot simply suggest that it is great being here, throw down $100,000 and risk losing it all because of our incompetence.

How about legislating that universities create offices of financial literacy to create a direct link between students and their loans. Financial literacy officers would be able to make it clear to students how to pay their loans, amounts, interest on the debt, and length of time they could be paying back their loans. If after year one, depending on the prospects for students with such a class rank, the student should be advised to withdraw and save a ton of money.

Mitch Daniels for all I have seen wants to solve this problem the best way. He has created an office similar to this at Purdue, and he was able to lower student loan defaults to the low single-digits across campus In addition, before students even choose a college, the FAFSA needs to be simplified, in order for students to more easily qualify for student aid. College is meant to be as accessible and affordable for everyone as functionally possible.

All facts should be disseminated in the media to which the student is most comfortable. Parents must also be informed, especially if they are forced to cosign. Actually, I would lift the cosign requirement and instead insist the university kick junior out of he is not in the top half of his class.

Lastly for some but firstly for me, colleges must have major skin in the game. Whether through incentives or punishment, universities need to pay for poor default and loan repayment rates. They can pay initial penalties via their massive endowments but after that, they need to be put out of the student loan or ISA business if their product is not usable in America.

Through federal or state governments, funding incentives could also be created for schools that make year over year improvements to their default and repayment rates.

On the other hand, schools could be forced to pay a small portion of student loan payments in years that their default/non-repayment are exceptionally high, in order to remain in the federal program. These incentives would help universities have a reason for concern about their students' success and ability to pay back their loans.

Chapter Conclusion

By understanding the roles of all the involved parties, one can consider ways in which each role can be better fit or incentivized to help make the system work better for all. Through some simple fixes (shortened FAFSA), and others more complex (government ISA program), efforts can be made to simplify and create opportunity for students, private entities, educational institutions, and the US Government. In all of these situations, the American College Student needs to be at the top of the consideration list.

Overall, one cannot emphasize enough the importance of this issue. Government student loan debt has tripled in the past ten years, and without making any changes it will not be getting better.

It is very uncertain what debt levels will be another decade from now. With more and more positions requiring degrees, the best thing America can do for its constituents is to offer simple, affordable, quality postsecondary education. Perhaps corporations should develop standardized essay and comprehensive examinations that can serve as markers in addition to GPAs to students willing to take such exams.

Most importantly though, the cost of education must be manageable and shared by more than just individual students and the American taxpayers. Through creating valuable synergies between students, educational institutions, the private sector, and the government, a much more efficient system can be implemented. Amen on that!

While students are ultimately responsible; it is also America's constitutional responsibility to create opportunity for its citizens.

I would encourage you to reflect on all those you know that are affected by student debt. This may be friends, family, yourself, or even your favorite barista at the local Starbucks down the street – all of whom are struggling to mitigate sometimes-unmanageable student loans.

Each individual may have a different story, but all have debt in common. Something that affects seven out of ten Americans should, and will soon be, a top priority.

As John Harvey of Forbes asserts, "Of course, one could rightly argue that no one forced them to go to college. They freely chose to extend their education beyond high-school leaving age and take on all this debt. But, it isn't as if they are taking out these loans to buy big-screen TVs or take Caribbean cruises. Moreover, at sixteen, seventeen, and eighteen years of age, these students are so positive on life, just as the smoking, the drug, and the credit card hustlers are getting them early, it is unfortunate but true that the marketing hustlers in our finest universities are convincing them to give up the debt for the greater life and the pleasure of enjoying their university. They never talk about the reality after graduation.

They are trying to increase what economists call human capital. They want to acquire new skills, learn new ways of thinking, and to develop specializations in particular areas of study. In short, they want to better themselves.

And, when they do that, we all gain. Nothing resounds more true than this idea. College education benefits more than just the student. It benefits more than the receiver of tuition, textbook manufacturers, loan servicers, or luxury off-campus housing complexes. When American citizens receive a college education, it benefits us all.

But, when it costs these impressionable people (millennials) their future, they realize they should have been taught better in college—but were not because their professors had an ideological bent. The lifetime earnings of so many people, mostly the young and vulnerable have been disrupted because the whole deal was and continues to be a fraud!

Chapter 10   Donald Trump Final Countdown on Student Loans

Trump knows the value of a great education

Donald Trump has often spoken about his position on the student loan crisis, and his opinion might surprise many. He has been interviewed many times on the issue and when he was interviewed Mr. Trump, slammed the federal government for profiting on federal student loans. "That's probably one of the only things the government shouldn't make money off. I think it's terrible that one of the only profit centers we have is student loans," said Trump.

As hard as it is for Americans who believe in government can imagine, Trump is right. As we I have discussed many times, the Federal Student Loan programs turned a profit of $41.3 billion in 2013 while many child-borrowers, who would rather be known as millennials were struggling to make their financial ends meet.

Creating Jobs

Donald Trump is a businessman and knows how to solve business problems. He knows that loans cannot be repaid when the borrower (student) cannot find a job. The Trump Plan as we have discussed from Chapter 1 to solve the student loan debt crisis begins by creating jobs in the private sector. Trump said: "I don't want to raise the minimum wage. I want to create jobs so people can get much more than that, so they can get five times what the minimum wage is," What college graduate wants to work for $15.00 per hour? It is ridiculous.

I have already discussed a number of Trump notions that would almost immediately solve the student loan debt crisis. None of those solutions suggested that the American taxpayer eat the debt.

Student Loan Forgiveness Programs

Even my children up to their ears in college debt are not looking for forgiveness. They got their degrees. They know they have to pay but with the job market as it is, they would like to be able to pay back their loans on a plan the interest charges of which are no more than the 1% that their parents earn on their income. Trump likes that plan. In many ways, we the parents still pay for those loans, fifteen years later.

0With the popularity of the Student Loan Forgiveness programs and enrollment into these programs skyrocketing, Trump could find it very hard to be vocal against these programs or face losing the student vote. Though Trump is a conservative, his position on student loans seems to be somewhat liberal, and we expect that, if elected, he will continue to promote the loan forgiveness programs.

By improving the job market as the Trump plan ensures, borrowers, such as my children would be able to make their payments rather than using their deferment and forbearance options until they expire. Trump feels that the government should not be profiting on student loans, then there is a possibility that he will elect to use the profits of this Obama takeover to expand the loan forgiveness programs as well as offering relief to borrowers who need immediate relief.

Nobody thinks student loan borrowers should have their debt 100% forgiven, but for God sakes, how about a plan that lets them pay as much as they can and get credit against the principal so that their largest bequethment, when these so indebted finally die, is not their debt.

Trump's Position on Student Loans

Yes, Donald Trump has a position on student loans. While some say that Trump has been extremely vague about his plans for student loans if elected, here's what we do know so far:

Trump has stated that he does not want the federal government profiting off of student loans any longer (and blames government for driving up tuition costs)
He thinks the Department of Education could "largely be eliminated," but did not elaborate on how the $28 billion spent on Pell Grants for students would be affected. He will make sure students and millennial graduates are OK!

He wants to restructure student loans but says government "can't forgive these loans" outright...

He wants to return student lending to private banks and away from the federal government (in order to improve salary data and allow students to make more informed decisions about whether the tuition costs are worth it)

He proposed tying new student loan decisions to the borrower's future job prospects, an assessment likely based on the student's major

He wants to punish colleges and universities who have not delivered to students financially when their students fail to repay their loans, adding that he wants colleges themselves to have "skin in the game" and would be on the hook if too many of their former students defaulted on their loans

Mr. Trump wants colleges to set more stringent standards for who is admitted, denying access to those it deems unlikely to succeed. Everybody has the right to pay up front and not be a financial burden on the rest of us.

Most of the issues covered in this book for hook or for crook are the way Donald Trump would solve them. If you do not believe so, let us know the issue and we will ask r. Trump to comment!

Chapter 11   Trump in the Final Analysis

Proves Donald Trump is our Best Presidential Choice

I began this book by noting that young and old borrowers alike owe collectively 1.3 trillion dollars of debt because they were sucked in and they took out public and private student loans. I noted this is and has been a bad Obama economy for the past eight years and thus as much as 30% of the borrowers have been defaulting on their loans. Yes, as bad as it once was, this number is rising every year.

Student debt is just one issue. They are all tied in. Issue by issue Donald Trump has the best solutions for America. Donald Trump is the only one who cares enough to say that he will make America great again.

Graduates with undergrad degrees and those with MBA's and other grad degrees as great as their prospects for employment once were, cannot make the minimum payments on their student loans.

It has gotten so bad that more and more older and former students with existing loans that have not been paid off, are entering their sixties. Some are now turning 62 years of age and, surprise—surprise, their social security checks are now being garnished by the government to pay off these old student loans.

It's worse than you can imagine. My research discovered an 82 year old gentleman who once guaranteed a friend's loan and he cannot escape the government's wrath. He has begun paying 40% of his social security check to pay off the loan. He is left with $750 per month. Something is wrong in America. He makes up the rest of his needs on welfare subsidies and food-stamps, where once he felt he could retire with dignity!

Many parents and future college students are questioning the value of a university education today when the loan brokers have to wait until retirement years to collect the debt from government payments intended to sustain life.

Students in the bottom 60% of the class with little prospect for work in their chosen field after graduation are wishing they could have that loan decision they made at 17 or 18 years old back again for a do-over.

They know their huge loans; many over $100,000 may very well ruin their lives. Nobody offered counselling on student debt and the negative impact it would have on the lives of so many of our young in America. Over 70% of graduates are on the hook to pay off student loans.

Where are the good jobs promised by the Universities for all the money borrowed? At the same time that most graduates cannot get jobs, the jobs they do get pay less.

The average salary of college graduates has gone down 10% in the past few years while inflation is growing at an ever faster clip. Moreover, 85% of college graduates from 2011 have had to swallow their pride and move home with mom and dad because they could not afford life on their own. It doesn't take a rocket scientist to call out: Houston, we have a problem! Donald Trump is well aware of the problem and he has the solutions.

Meanwhile nobody is talking about the Universities permitting more and more foreign students into their programs. When they graduate; guess whose jobs they take? A major source of H-1B visas (college graduates) is international students from U.S. university campuses. Though like most of us Trump is OK on legal aliens, he is not OK in seeing legal aliens (foreign nationals with allegiance to another country) be the preferred class of graduates getting the best jobs in America.

The reason corporations hire them before Americans is they are a ready source of cheap labor. Even legal, they work for less hoping to be sponsored by corporations for a few additional years until they can get a green card and permanently take jobs from Americans.

Universities not only sell their foreign national graduates to corporations, they also hire more than their fair share of professors from the foreign national community many who have just received graduate degrees from American Universities.

Universities also fire existing faculty and replace them with younger foreign national professors willing to work for less money. After achieving outstanding evaluations, I was fired from Marywood University for a cost-cutting restructuring and my replacement had recently graduated from the University of Alexandria in Egypt. Was that just a coincidence? Marywood did not open up its employment dossier to me but what seems to be is most often what is.

Smaller Universities will even outsource the legal part of the visa work to assure the foreign applicant gets a six-year H-1B visa. They will contract with immigration law firms and pay up to $10,000 or more per faculty member depending on the complexity of the case for the purpose of hiring a new faculty member who will work cheap. They do not care about American faculty members and they do not care about American students either.

Do cheap-wage foreign-speaking non-citizen faculty have any effect on the quality of education our children receive?

It is really tough for Americans to get hired in US Universities since our Congress permits an unlimited number of foreign nationals to be hired as professors or staff at US Universities. Additionally, colleges also love to hire part timers at about 1/10 the pay rate as full-timers. Meanwhile graduating students not getting jobs to help them pay off their massive student debt? Can it be that their education was not as advertised?

Millennial graduates continue to need parents to survive.

With more and more former students not being able to survive without their parents, this also has an impact on the student borrower's ability to ever break away. Purchasing a home is out of the question as the college loan is already bigger than the mortgage would be. This is already having a major effect on the housing market and it will continue for

years to come. Who will buy America's newest homes if not
the young?

Solutions: Where there is a will...

No solution is simple. With 30% or more former students
ultimately defaulting on their loans, and many more trapped
in a financial hell-hole from which they can never escape,
Congress can certainly create a better way to help the
borrower, the housing market, and the taxpayer, all at the
same time.

In a Donald Trump-style payback plan, I would suggest that
Congress assure that in times when saving earns just a
percent or two interest, student lenders should have their
interest rates capped at the same interest rates.

Use a Donald Trump payback style

Then, I would recommend putting together a progressive
payback schedule (like the progressive income tax) based on
adjusted gross income. Students do not want to default but
part-time jobs do not permit them to pay back huge amounts
every month. Every borrower with income or on
government payments should have to pay something.
Nobody should pay less than 1% of their income per year.
Likewise 95% or 110% of income is way too high.

On a graduated "progressive scale," I would start the
maximum rate of payment at 5% for the lowest income
borrowers and then take it up to 15% for those in default
with huge debts who have begun to do quite well. Of course

in no instance would anybody have to pay more than the minimum monthly payment for the loan even if they could afford it. The road out of default should be rewarded.

To help pay for the program, I would also set up a fund for any taxpayer to check off on their tax form from $1.00 up to any amount of their refund and have it directed towards the paying down of all student loans or for specific students. We do this for campaign donations so why not for student loans. I have other recommendations and the one immediately below may be considered somewhat controversial.

Some skin in the game for colleges

All of this money that former students have paid and will pay over the years has already gone into the coffers of Universities across the nation, who seemingly have no skin in the game. They got paid for their "service" up front and have never been asked to look back until Donald Trump becomes President. They have pocketed the money for many students who have never been able to get a job—ever.

And, since the products of the universities, the students, as a rule have not been able to achieve the American Dream as promised by the Admissions Counselors, and since such universities encourage foreign students to take jobs in the US upon graduation and they hire foreign faculty when Americans are available, universities cannot be left out of the solution.

Their admission departments and "loan" departments have actually created the problem. They keep seventeen year old prospective students in the dark as half of the graduating students are not even aware that they have massive debt from a loan that they signed years earlier. Universities are a part of the problem. In this regard, I would ask the Congress to enact legislation to make them part of the Donald Trump solution, by providing the following:

1. Based on their student default rate, collect a fee of 5% of gross revenue to 15% (same rates as student payback) that is applied to paying down all student loans from their university graduates. The minimum payment would be a factor of the default rate for the institution and the percentage of gross revenue. The exact formula will need some work.

2. Limit the number of foreign students admitted until the unemployment rate is 3%.

3. Cap the number of graduates permitted to obtain work visas after graduation to a very small / reasonable number. Until the dent problem is solved, require student visa holders to go home.

4. Limit the number of H-1B visas for faculty to a very small number-- 5%. It is currently unlimited.

5. Assure the H-1B faculty member on worker visa returns to his or her home country after 6 years.

6. Those with worker visas should not do not be able to get in line for green cards or citizenship. After their visa time, they must go home.

7. Reduce all non-University H-1B visas from 85,000 or whatever the limit is du jour by 90% until the unemployment rate goes to 3%.

8. Come up with a payment plan in addition to the above in which a certain percentage, say 5% per year of the endowment is used to pay off student debt. To make it fair, this also would be based on the default rate for the institution. An endowment is typically a large fund that is amassed by universities and other institutions from the kind donations / bequeathals of dedicated alumni.

The dollars in university endowments are staggering and could pay off the country's entire student debt. For example, Harvard University alone, with its 380 years' worth of alumni to hit up, boasts an endowment of $36 billion. Apple Inc.'s famously large cash hoard is just $21 billion. Yes, Harvard has more cash than Apple while students are in loan default trying to pay off their Harvard loans. Both Yale University and Stanford University's endowments are also larger than Apple's cash hoard, and Princeton University is not too far behind.

9. **The Trump Debt Payoff Plan**. Use just 5% of the proceeds from the Trump plan to balance the budget to pay off the debt. That is all that would be needed. Just 5% of the Trump balanced budget plan will pay off the entire student debt load in eight years. The notable economists who have created our terrible economic performance in the past eight years have already weighed in that they do not like the Trump plan for the national debt. From my perspective, these are the people who failed America. They have already proven they cannot handle the job.

Many who study Mr. Trump already know that as president, Donald Trump is considering selling off $16 trillion worth of U.S. government assets in order to fulfill his pledge to eliminate the national debt in eight years, a senior adviser with the campaign, Barry Bennett said recently. This is a

great idea. How about adding another $1.3 trillion to the
total repayment plans to handle all existing student debt.

"The United States government owns more real estate than
anybody else, more land than anybody else, more energy
than anybody else," Bennett announced. "We can get rid of
government buildings we're not using, we can extract the
energy from government lands, we can do all kinds of things
to extract value from the assets that we hold."

In a wide-ranging interview with The Washington Post,
Trump said he would get rid of the $19 trillion national debt
"over a period of eight years."

10. **Use Trump's America-First Fossil Fuel Plan**. Take a
nice cut in fees from granting permission opening up all US
oil lands. While Obama administration headlines have
reported declining oil, gas, and coal prices, those declines do
not deter from the fact that U.S. energy resources are very
valuable to our domestic economic growth. The most recent
government estimate of those benefits was a 2012
Congressional Budget Office (CBO) study, produced at the
request of the House Budget Committee.

This study analyzed federal lease revenues that could be
expected to arise from a proposal to open federal lands and
waters to oil, gas, and coal extraction. Donald Trump is
ready to bring this in right away and it will more than pay
for outstanding student debt. Remember we need $1.3
trillion to pay it all off. Look at the results from the US study
below. Without even using anything from the Trump Debt
Payoff Plan, taking advantage of the fossil fuels on public
lands can deliver great returns to the public if managed by a
businessman such as President Donald Trump. Check this
out:

GDP increase:

- ✓ $127 billion annually for the next seven years.
- ✓ $663 billion annually in the next thirty years.
- ✓ $20.7 trillion cumulative increase in economic activity over the next thirty-seven years.

These estimates include "spillover" effects, or gains that extend from one location to another location. For example, increased oil production in the Gulf of Mexico might lead to more automobile purchases that would increase economic activity in Michigan.

Spillover effects would add an estimated $69 billion annually in the next seven years and $178 billion over thirty years.

Only a president who knows nothing about business would say no to such a deal. Both Obama and Hillary have said no already to increasing the benefits of fossil fuels for America and Americans. It is what is. There are more benefits:

Jobs increase:

- ✓ 552,000 jobs annually over the next seven years.
- ✓ Roughly 2.7 million jobs annually over the next thirty years.

Jobs gains would be not only in fields directly related to oil, gas, and coal but more than 75% of the jobs would be in high-wage, high-skill employment like health care, education, professional fields, and the arts.

Is there anybody in American interested in a raise? Here is what the productive use of energy will do for the wages in the country.

Wage increase:

- ✓ $32 billion increase in annual wages over the next seven years.
- ✓ $163 billion annually between seven and thirty years.
- ✓ $5.1 trillion cumulative increase over thirty-seven years.

There is no question that after ten years of negatives, Americans all need a raise. Despite how much money we feed the government, their statistics are always way behind the current year. Nonetheless, experts were able to learn a lot about wages.

There were virtually no well-paying jobs created during the eight years of the Obama Administration, though part-time and low-paying jobs have been created. Thus, according to the US Census Bureau, the typical American family income was $53,657 in 2014, down about $800 from $54,462 a year earlier.

The trajectory has been down for all of the Obama years but he won't tell you so and Hillary Clinton keeps insisting that

America is at its greatest and does not have to get great again.

What's worse is that these numbers are far below the wage peak set in 1999. This is the big reason why Americans are gloomy about the economy six years into the faux recovery. It is not getting better and that is why Donald Trump is needed immediately. Whites saw incomes decline 1.7%, while blacks, Hispanics and Asians saw no significant difference.

Median income remains lower than it was in 2007, Census said. Precise comparisons, however, are now difficult because the government has not figured out how to provide proper data. The earnings of women who work full time were essentially the same as they were in 2007, while men's earnings were 2.2% lower.

Democratic candidates plan to solve the problem by raising the minimum wage. Ask yourself, if somebody making $53,000 be at minimum wage? Of course not, so the Democrat plan will not help the middle class at all.

Moreover, by increasing the minimum wage, seniors on fixed income will be the major victims as everything will cost more and seniors know that the Democrats when they hold the presidency, do not give seniors any raises in Social Security but they do raise Medicare rates.

Republicans want to spur job creation by lowering taxes and shedding regulations. Donald Trump wants to revitalize American industry, and renew our leadership in energy. His plan can give everybody a wage increase without government involvement. A better economy also produces more revenue for the government to help us be fiscally responsible.

Increase in tax revenue:

- ✓ $3.9 trillion increase in federal tax revenues over thirty-seven years.
- ✓ $1.9 trillion in state and local tax revenues over thirty-seven years.
- ✓ $24 billion annual federal tax revenue over the next seven years, $126 billion annually thereafter.
- ✓ $10 billion annual state and local tax revenue over the next seven years, $61 billion annually thereafter.

Why does Hillary's plan ignore these facts?

It is so obvious that we need a good business mind in the white house to be able to achieve these gains from energy and other areas of the economy. Yet, Hillary Clinton is very pleased with Obama's results. Ask her why. Here are three likely answers"

1. She did not think of it
2. She hates fossil fuels like oil and gas and coal
3. She hates corporations that create jobs

If she had another good thought, it would be lonesome.

Chapter 12   The Trump Plan Reduces the # of Additional Student Debtors

Should students take on all the risk?

Sam Clovis is the national co-chair and policy director of Trump's campaign. He has presented a number of Trump ideas that are still a work-in-progress. Few things regarding student loan debt are final as this matter is too important to rush.

Clovis said the Trump campaign expects higher education to be a major issue in the fall general election. He is right. Hillary will try to rob the treasury and increase taxes on the middle class to create a massive give-away. Trump knows there are better ways and we have already discussed many of them.

[A number of the notions in this chapter have come from the web site--insidehighered.com.]

One proposal being prepared sounds very appealing. It would alter the current system of student loans in which students have all the risk. It would force all colleges to share the risk of such loans and make it harder for those wanting to major in the liberal arts at non-elite institutions to obtain loans. Statistics show that the latter are less likely to be able to pay off a student loan as their incomes if they can get jobs would be quite low. This is a groundbreaking notion.

Trump is well aware that a number of his ideas might face a skeptical Congress. Nonetheless his ideas could gain considerable attention if Trump uses them to parry with his Democratic opponent. One simply must ask if Congress is so smart in evaluating proposals: "Why has it not solved the problem?"

From a parent's perspective, Congress is the greatest enemy of parents caught in the student loan mess. It was Congress that created the law that even students with no means of paying back a loan—those who are in fact bankrupt, still must carry that loan on their backs until the day the student loan holder dies.

Mr. Clovis is a tenured professor of economics at Morningside College, a small private college in Iowa, who is currently on leave to work for the Trump campaign.

Some of Clovis' recent pronouncements on Trump policies have been widely criticized by the same Washington experts and bureaucrats who have been advising Obama. They find Trump's work as unworkable or unrealistic. Yet, they have failed America for eight long years.

Clovis said he expects some higher education leaders to react the same way as Trump outlines these ideas in the fall campaign. He said the campaign remains open to ideas as long as they put the emphasis on student success in ways that have more impact than the failed efforts of past administrations.

First off, Clovis made clear that the Trump campaign will fight and not endorse Hillary Clinton's proposal for debt-free public higher education or the Bernie Sanders plan for free public higher education. The response on those ideas will be "unequivocally no," Clovis said. "How do you pay for that? It's absurd on its surface." Trump has ideas to pay for everything, including the massive student debt load.

Further, Trump also rejects President Obama's proposals for a state-federal partnership to make community college free for new high school graduates. Community colleges are "damn near free" now, and "almost anyone can afford community college," he said. It is funny that Obama and Hillary are teaming up again on solutions for problems that have been here for each of the past eight years. Where were their solutions?

Big Changes for Student Loans

The Trump campaign is working on a complete overhaul of the federal student loan system. Few Americans felt comfortable when Obama got rid of Sallie Mae and then made about $40 billion on the backs of students. Trump is moving the government out of lending and restoring that role to private banks, and places like Sallie Mae. This was how things were before President Clinton partially and President Obama fully shifted loan origination from private lenders to the government.

"We think it should be marketplace and market driven," he said. Local banks should be lending to local students, he said, but colleges should be playing a role in determining loan worthiness on factors that go beyond family income.

Further, Clovis said that all colleges should have "skin in the game" and share the risk associated with student loans.

Many in Congress (and not just Republicans) have voiced support for that idea.

Unfortunately, Democrats are looking to get some favors for their constituencies which are almost always non-white. The forgotten white man is still not remembered by Democrats. The Democrats are arguing already that some institutions -- historically black colleges, for example -- should be exempt, given their histories of educating many students from low-income families who may not have the financial resources of others. But Clovis said that the principle of colleges sharing risk must apply to all institutions.

Further, the Trump Plan recognizes that the risk needs to be substantial enough to change the way colleges decide whether to admit students, and which programs they offer.

Clovis said he hoped many colleges would continue to provide remediation for those unprepared for college-level work, although he said that he preferred the term "student success programs" to remediation.

He noted that colleges should not be admitting students that they aren't confident can graduate in a reasonable time frame and find jobs. There is little sense for somebody who is a high risk of not finishing college to become engrossed in debt.

Therefore, those who decide who gets student loans, when looking at those students with less emphasis on parent contributions and the Free Application for Federal Student Aid, need to consider more of "a partnership" between the student, the bank and the college. "We think if the college has real skin in the game, if it will change its model."

And these reforms would make it legitimate for colleges and banks to make decisions in part on students' prospective majors and their likely earnings after graduation, he said.

"If you are going to study 16th-century French art, more power to you. I support the arts," Clovis said. "But you are not going to get a job."

A college should factor that in when deciding on a student's loan eligibility, and the requirement that colleges share the risk would be a powerful incentive to do so, Clovis added.

"If you get into the esoteric aspects of a particular art field, you have to know that those are the circumstances," he said. The moral of the story is that colleges may not get a new student if they tell the student the truth and they prevent likely defaulters from getting loans. So, they give up something while a prospective student gets a way to figure out how to move ahead without such heavy lifelong loan drag.

Trump campaign is not against the liberal arts. The fact is that liberal arts positions are few and far between and in most cases, they pay less than the hard science. "The liberal arts education is the absolute foundation to success in life," Clovis said, adding that he hoped business and engineering and health professions and education students would include liberal arts courses in their college educations. But it is a different thing altogether, Clovis said, to focus on such fields. "If you choose to major in the liberal arts, there are issues associated with that." Not ever getting a job in your field, and becoming a bartender are two of the issues.

There may be colleges that decide they would be happy backing loans for students who study the liberal arts. That gives college's more skin in the game if they think their education is worth the risk. A prestigious college could legitimately decide that anyone it graduates -- regardless of major -- will do well in life, and so go ahead with approving the borrowing. "If you go to Harvard, you can major in anything you want, and once you get in the door, you'll be OK," Clovis said, so such a college might be fine with its students borrowing to study the liberal arts. "But not all colleges are in the same system," he said.

Community Colleges, For-Profits and More

The Trump campaign would encourage community colleges, in much the same fashion as four-year colleges, to focus on serving students who can succeed. Helping students succeed is also a worthwhile effort but minimizing risk in the loan area is paramount for both the student and the institution. Based on his research, Clovis said, there is much for community colleges to be proud of. They do a great job in job-training programs for examples as well as preparing students for year three and four of a four year degree.

For Profits need to be studied further according to Clovis. "The business model for for-profit higher education is quite different" from that of nonprofit colleges. The Trump campaign is working to figure out how to propose improvements for the for-profit education sector.

The Obama administration has been widely seen as being very tough on the sector, and many Republicans in Congress have accused the administration of overstepping its authority in this area. Clovis, given a chance to weigh in on such criticism, chose to pass. He said the focus of the campaign's ideas on higher education was public and private nonprofit higher education.

Trump's advisor is a fan of nonprofit colleges that adopt some strategies from for-profit models. For example, he praised Regis University, where he once taught. The institution has a traditional residential campus in Colorado, but a much larger student body enrolled online.

Remove the Department of Education.

Ron Paul and Donald Trump both want the Department of Education eliminated. "Once we get into office, we're going to take a hard look at the Department of Education," Clovis said. "There are lots of things that serve people well, but there are many operations that do not.

In wrapping up his discussion, Clovis noted that College administrators should be speaking out in defense of free speech, he said. "We need leadership that says that one side does not get to dictate what is said." Donald Trump is a free speech advocate. Many campuses want to shot down all free speech related to the Trump Presidential campaign. I wonder where Hillary is on Free Speech.

There is no question that Trump's plan can help the Student debt issue in two ways. 1. By helping those with minimal chances of success in college to avoid the massive life-ruining debt of massive student loans. Paying off the loan debt through a number of clever techniques, and permitting students to be removed from default when they pay anything.

The problem is real and Trump will solve It is definitely not a myth. A friend of mine's son just completed his Masters in sociology at a private four-year institution where he also obtained his BA. His total education debt is now almost $190,000. His best job offer is for $27,000. He would have done as well or better with a teaching certificate. Students and their parents really do need to look at the probable jobs and salaries of their chosen field before taking on that kind of debt. Amen!

LETS GO PUBLISH! Books by Brian Kelly:
(sold at www.bookhawkers.com Amazon.com, and Kindle.).

LETS GO PUBLISH! is proud to announce that more AS/400 and Power i books are becoming available to help you inexpensively address your AS/400 and Power i education and training needs: Our general titles precede specific AS/400 and other technology books. Check out these great patriotic books which precede the tech books in the list.

101 Secrets How to be a High Information Voter
You do not have to be a low-information voter.

Why Trump?
You Already Know… But, this book will tell you anyway

Saving America The Trump Way!
A book that tells you how President Donald Trump will help Merica dn Americans wind up on top

The US Immigration Fix
It's all in here. You won't want to put it down

I had a Dream IBM Could be #1 Again
The title is self-explanatory

Whatever Happened to the IBM AS/400?
The question is answered in this nee book.

Great Moments in Penn State Football Check out the particulars of this great book at bookhawkers.com.

Great Moments in Notre Dame Football Check out the particulars of this great book at bookhawkers.com or www.notredamebooks.com

WineDiets.Com Presents The Wine Diet Learn how to lose weight while having fun. Four specific diets and some great anecdotes fill this book with fun and the opportunity to lose weight in the process.

Wilkes-Barre, PA; Return to Glory Wilkes-Barre City's return to glory begins with dreams and ideas. Along with plans and actions, this equals leadership.

The Lifetime Guest Plan. This is a plan which if deployed today would immediately solve the problem of 60 million illegal aliens in the United States.

Geoffrey Parsons' Epoch… The Land of Fair Play Better than the original. The greatest re-mastering of the greatest book ever written on American Civics. It was built for all Americans as the best govt. design in the history of the world.

The Bill of Rights 4 Dummmies! This is the best book to learn about your rights. Be the first, to have a "Rights Fest" on your block. You will win for sure!

Sol Bloom's Epoch …Story of the Constitution This work by Sol Bloom was written to commemorate the Sesquicentennial celebration of the Constitution. It has been remastered by Lets Go Publish! – An excellent read!

The Constitution 4 Dummmies! This is the best book to learn about the Constitution. Learn all about the fundamental laws of America.

America for Dummmies!
All Americans should read to learn about this great country.

Just Say No to Chris Christie for President two editions – I & II
Discusses the reasons why Chris Christie is a poor choice for US President

The Federalist Papers by Hamilton, Jay, Madison w/ intro by Brian Kelly
Complete unabridged, easier to read version of the original Federalist Papers

Companion to Federalist Papers by Hamilton, Jay, Madison w/ intro by Brian Kelly
This small, inexpensive book will help you navigate the Federalist Papers

Kill the Republican Party! (2013 edition and edition #2)
Demonstrates why the Republican Party must be abandoned by conservatives

Bring On the American Party!
Demonstrates how conservatives can be free from the party of wimps by starting its own national party called the American Party.

No Amnesty! No Way!
In addition to describing the issue in detail, this book offers a real solution.

Saving America
This how-to book is about saving our country using strong mercantilist principles. These same principles that helped the country from its founding.

RRR:
A unique plan for economic recovery and job creation

Kill the EPA
The EPA seems to hate mankind and love nature. They are also making it tough for asthmatics to breathe and for those with malaria to live. It's time they go.

Obama's Seven Deadly Sins.
In the Obama Presidency, there are many concerns about the long-term prospects and sustainability of the country. We examine each of the President's seven deadliest sins in detail, offering warnings and a number of solutions. Be careful. Book may nudge you to move to Canada or Europe.

Taxation Without Representation Second Edition
At the time of the Boston Tea Party, there was no representation. Now, there is no representation again but there are "representatives."

Healthcare Accountability
Who should pay for your healthcare? Whose healthcare should you pay for? Is it a lifetime free ride on others or should those once in need of help have to pay it back when their lives improve?

Jobs! Jobs! Jobs!
Where have all the American Jobs gone and how can we get them back?

Other IBM I Technical Books

The All Everything Operating System:
Story about IBM's finest operating system; its facilities; how it came to be.

The All-Everything Machine
Story about IBM's finest computer server.

Chip Wars
The story of ongoing wars between Intel and AMD and upcoming wars between Intel and IBM. Book may cause you to buy / sell somebody's stock.

Can the AS/400 Survive IBM?
Exciting book about the AS/400 in a System i5 World.

The IBM i Pocket SQL Guide.
Complete Pocket Guide to SQL as implemented on System i5. A must have for SQL developers new to System i5. It is very compact yet very comprehensive and it is example driven. Written in a part tutorial and part reference style, Tons of SQL coding samples, from the simple to the sublime.

The IBM i Pocket Query Guide.
If you have been spending money for years educating your Query users, and you find you are still spending, or you've given up, this book is right for you. This one QuikCourse covers all Query options.

The IBM I Pocket RPG & RPG IV Guide.
Comprehensive RPG & RPGIV Textbook -- Over 900 pages. This is the one RPG book to have if you are not having more than one. All areas of the language covered smartly in a convenient sized book Annotated PowerPoint's available for self-study (extra fee for self-study package)

The IBM I RPG Tutorial and Lab Guide – Recently Revised.
Your guide to a hands-on Lab experience. Contains CD with Lab exercises and PowerPoint's. Great companion to the above textbook or can be used as a standalone for student Labs or tutorial purposes

The IBM i Pocket Developers' Guide.
Comprehensive Pocket Guide to all of the AS/400 and System i5 development tools - DFU, SDA, etc. You'll also get a big bonus with chapters on Architecture, Work Management, and Subfile Coding.

The IBM i Pocket Database Guide.
Complete Pocket Guide to System i5 integrated relational database (DB2/400) – physical and logical files and DB operations - Union, Projection, Join, etc. Written in a part tutorial and part reference style. Tons of DDS coding samples.

Getting Started with The WebSphere Development Studio Client for System i5 (WDSc). Focus is on client server and the Web. Includes CODE/400, VisualAge RPG, CGI, WebFacing, and WebSphere Studio. Case study continues from the Interactive Book.

The System i5 Pocket WebFacing Primer.
This book gets you started immediately with WebFacing. A sample case study is used as the basis for a conversion to WebFacing. Interactive 5250 application is WebFaced in a case study form before your eyes.

Getting Started with WebSphere Express Server for IBM i Step-by-Step Guide for Setting up Express Servers
A comprehensive guide to setting up and using WebSphere Express. It is filled with examples, and structured in a tutorial fashion for easy learning.

The WebFacing Application Design & Development Guide:
Step by Step Guide to designing green screen IBM i apps for the Web. Both a systems design guide and a developers guide. Book helps you understand how to design and develop Web applications using regular RPG or COBOL programs.

The System i5 Express Web Implementer's Guide.
Your one stop guide to ordering, installing, fixing, configuring, and using WebSphere Express, Apache, WebFacing, System i5 Access for Web, and HATS/LE.

Joomla! Technical Books

Best Damn Joomla Tutorial Ever
Learn Joomla! By example.

Best Damn Joomla Intranet Tutorial Ever
This book is the only book that shows you how to use Joomla on a corporate intranet.

Best Damn Joomla Template Tutorial Ever
This book teaches you step-by step how to work with templates in Joomla!

Best Damn Joomla Installation Guide Ever
Teaches you how to install Joomla! On all major platforms besides IBM i.

Best Damn Blueprint for Building Your Own Corporate Intranet.
This excellent timeless book helps you design a corporate intranet for any platform while using Joomla as its basis.
4
IBM i PHP & MySQL Installation & Operations Guide
How to install and operate Joomla! on the IBM i Platform

IBM i PHP & MySQL Programmers Guide
programs for IBM i